MW00466744

UNTO DEATH

*Martyrdom, Missions, and the
Maturity of the Church*

DALTON THOMAS

UNTO DEATH
Martyrdom, Missions, and the Maturity of the Church
DALTON THOMAS

Copyright © 2012 Dalton Thomas
All rights reserved.

ISBN: 978-0-9876633-0-6

For more resources: http://daltonthomas.org

Cover and Design by Carter Romo

Published by Maskilim Publishing
http://maskilimpublishing.com

Unless marked otherwise, Scripture quotations are from *The Holy Bible, English Standard Version®* (ESV®), Copyright © 2001 by Crossway, a publishing ministry of Good News Publishers. Used by permission. All rights reserved.

All italics within quotations have been added by this author for emphasis, unless otherwise indicated in a footnote. In addition, some personal pronouns in Scripture have been capitalized by the author.

The world is a dangerous place for Christians. All the more so for those who spearhead the gospel into spiritual strongholds where Satan has exerted his control, almost unchallenged, for centuries. As the name of Christ advances, there will always be fierce demonic backlash. How then, should we, the Church, respond to such hostility? Do we fearfully shrink back, or do we boldly proceed? Truly, our response is defined by how deeply we treasure the pearl (Matthew 13:45-46). I appreciate the way *Unto Death* repeatedly returns us to Christ and encourages us not only to count the cost, but to joyfully pay it.

DAVID SITTON
President of To Every Tribe Ministries

In a day when many best-selling Christian books focus on living in such a way as to get the most out of *this life*, Dalton Thomas skillfully articulates the biblical mentality needed to live fully for the age *which is yet to come*. *Unto Death* challenges, convicts, and comforts all who would willingly embrace Paul's words, "to live is Christ and to die is gain."

SCOTT VOLK
Pastor of FIRE Church
Charlotte, North Carolina

I was deeply challenged as I read *Unto Death*. Dalton Thomas has issued a vital apostolic call and I could only ask the Father to prepare my own heart for such obedience. We live in momentous times when this will surely be required of all those who love the Lord Jesus.

CHARLES P. SCHMITT
Immanuel's Church
Silver Spring, Maryland

Unto Death is a trumpet call to believers everywhere to lay down our lives—even potentially *literally*—for the high honor of making Jesus famous in all the Earth! Joy and soberness mark this book on martyrdom as Dalton portrays both the theology and practice of following Jesus in total abandonment. Teachings like this one *must* be embraced if we desire to see the powers of darkness vanquished and the glorious Bride enter into her finest hour at the end of the age. Surely nothing is impossible for a generation that believes and walks this message out.

ANDY BYRD
Director of Fire and Fragrance Ministries
YWAM, University of the Nations, Kona, HI

Written with extraordinary biblical clarity, and drawing from a great "cloud of witnesses" spanning Church history, Dalton Thomas's *Unto Death* is a tour de force on the subject of martyrdom, suffering, and the glory of God. It is a clarion blast to the saints in these last days—a rare word that must be imbibed, not merely read.

BRYAN PURTLE
Pastor/Preacher in the Antioch Prayer Society
Kansas City, Missouri

Jesus told us—in no uncertain terms—that unless we are willing to sacrifice everything, *including our own lives*, for the sake of the Gospel, we cannot be His disciples (Luke 14:26). As the majority of the Church today preaches an utter perversion of the true Gospel, *Unto Death* is one of the most important, timely, and prophetic books of this generation. If you genuinely desire to be a disciple of Jesus and gain a deeper understanding of the undiluted Gospel message as it was proclaimed by the early Church, then you absolutely must read this book.

JOEL RICHARDSON
Author of Islamic Antichrist

Unto Death is a bold reminder that the call to follow Jesus is no less radical today than it was 2,000 years ago when Jesus charged His first disciples to deny themselves, take up their cross, and follow Him. Yet many who would follow Jesus today have misunderstood this to be the *goal* of the Christian life—that somehow, some day, they might grow to the point where they would be willing to die for Him. But strikingly, Jesus declares "death to self" to be the starting point, the *beginning* of the Christian life. This life which we long to adventurously and courageously live *right now* is not possible until all allegiances to the world are renounced and our own death embraced. What a bold and stirring word! *Unto Death* is written with the clarity and conviction that can only come from one who is living its message fully. This is a must-read.

KEITH COWART, D. Min. Asbury Theological Seminary
Lead Pastor of Christ Community Church
Columbus, Georgia

Dalton's thorough research, articulate message, and prophetic insight define the pages of this book as a clear trumpet call to a generation willing to surrender their lives to follow Jesus—even if it be "unto death." May this timely message go forth with speed and unction!

SEAN FEUCHT
Founder of BURN 24/7

To Tom And Kimberly Roof

The first missionaries I ever met.

CONTENTS

ACKNOWLEDGMENTS

Joanna Silveira, Adam Kinunen, Carter Romo, and Nicola Walsh made vital contributions to this book. I am thankful for their input and grateful for their friendship.

SUFFERING. PERSECUTION. MARTYRDOM.

These are not words we regularly hear coming from the Sunday pulpit in the Western Church. Yet despite the popular teachings which promise a life of health, wealth, and blessings—and one which is *devoid of* trials and tribulations—the Scriptures are abundantly clear that *all believers* should fully expect and embrace the prospect of experiencing persecution, suffering, and martyrdom for the sake of the Gospel.[1] It can be biblically maintained, in fact, that these are some of the *foremost characteristics of authentic Christian living.* Did not Christ Himself assure us that, unless we suffer with Him, we cannot reign with Him?[2] How rightly then C.S. Lewis argued that the question is not why some "believing people suffer, but *why some do not.*"[3]

1   John 15:20; 1 Thessalonians 3:3-4; 2 Thessalonians 1:4-5; 2 Timothy 3:12; Colossians 1:24; Philippians 1:21; Revelation 12:11

2   2 Timothy 2:11-12

3   C.S. Lewis, *The Problem of Pain. The Complete C.S. Lewis Signature Classics,* (New York: Harper One, 2002), 611.

Nonetheless, for much of the Western Church caught in the self-promoting grip of materialism and comfort, a Christian experience which includes suffering and persecution is completely foreign and utterly resisted.

Yet there are some who have been burdened with a *godly discontent*—blood-bought saints who recognize that this sort of "cheap grace" was entirely alien to the first-century Church. Among these, there is a cry rising up in the Body of Christ to be delivered from such a polluted and plastic religion, and a longing for an apostolic faith akin to that of the early Church. There is, indeed, a sense that something has got to give in this generation to reverse the culture of easy believism, comfort, and convenience.

In the book of Revelation, we get a glimpse into the anticipation and hope of the saints who willingly follow the Lamb "whithersoever he goeth" in the last days. Revelation 12:11 succinctly reveals that the disciples of Christ in the last days will experience great victory as they overcome the enemy by the "blood of the Lamb" and the "word of their testimony," *even as* they lose their lives for the sake of love. These will be those who do "not love their lives so much as to shrink from death."

We have to wonder—if the apostolic embrace of suffering and death seems so deeply strange and uncomfortable to us—do we actually possess the same faith as that of the early Church? Do we follow the same Lamb?

As the Church, we must recognize that the Great Commission of the Gospel is at stake. Gripped by fear and an overriding goal of self-preservation, few Christians today will pursue dangerous or even "risky" situations to advance the Kingdom of God. Even despite great world-wide spiritual need, when the ancient path of suffering and possibly even martyrdom is placed before us, most of us will either turn a blind eye or shrink back in fear. Missionary great, Hudson Taylor, once wrote that "unless there is the element of extreme risk in our exploits for God, there is no need for faith."[4] It is time for the Church, once more, to embrace the mindset that *risk, for the Kingdom of God, is right.*

Unfortunately, however, because many of us subtly but erroneously believe that *God's chief end is our satisfaction*, we mistakenly assume that any difficult path, particularly something that may lead to suffering or our "untimely" deaths, is too foolish to be right. This theology stands in direct opposition to the Word of God and the testimonies of countless martyr-saints who understood firsthand that, "when Christ calls a man, *He bids him come and die.*"[5]

When will the Gospel again become what it once was—foolish and dangerous, yes, but wholly worth our everything? The Church now stands at a crossroads. How will we answer His call?

Consider the following letter written by an American college student nearly sixty years ago who had been converted to *communism* in Mexico. Today, we could easily imagine it representing the same spirit that energizes radical Muslim terrorists around the world. The purpose of the letter was to explain to his fiancée why he had to break off their engagement. I challenge you as you read it, *and reread it*, to consider the manner in which you embrace the *holy cause.* Can you relate to such a level of abandonment? Can we, as believers, describe our lives in a similar fashion?

4   Quote attributed to Hudson Taylor, source unknown.
5   Dietrich Bonhoeffer, *The Cost of Discipleship,* (New York: Macmillan, 1963), 99.

We Communists have a high casualty rate. We're the ones who get shot and hung and lynched and tarred and feathered and jailed and slandered, and ridiculed and fired from our jobs, and in every other way made as uncomfortable as possible. A certain percentage of us get killed or imprisoned. We live in virtual poverty. We turn back to the party every penny we make above what is absolutely necessary to keep us alive. We Communists don't have the time or the money for many movies, or concerts, or T-bone steaks, or decent homes and new cars. We've been described as fanatics. We are fanatics. Our lives are dominated by one great overshadowing factor: *the struggle for world communism.*

We Communists have a philosophy of life which no amount of money could buy. We have a cause to fight for, a definite purpose in life. We subordinate our petty, personal selves into a great movement of humanity, and if our personal lives seem hard, or our egos appear to suffer through subordination to the party, then we are adequately compensated by the thought that each of us in his small way is contributing to something new and true and better for mankind. There is one thing in which I am in dead earnest and that is the Communist cause. It is my life, my business, my religion, my hobby, my sweetheart, my wife and mistress, my bread and meat. I work at it in the daytime and dream of it at night. Its hold on me grows, not lessens as time goes on. Therefore, I cannot carry on a friendship, a love affair, or even a conversation without relating it to this force which both drives and guides my life. I evaluate people, books, ideas, and actions according to how they affect the Communist cause and by their attitude toward it. I've already been in jail because of my ideas and if necessary, I'm ready to go before a firing squad.[6]

It is my prayer that the saints who read this book will be challenged to embrace such a radical philosophy of life and

6   William Macdonald, *True Discipleship*, (Ontario, CA: Gospel Folio Press, 2003), 43-44.

death. May God deliver us all from the "dread asbestos of other things"[7] and set our hearts aflame to give everything, even our very lives, for the sake of love.

Brian Kim
IHOP–KC Senior Team
Executive Director, Antioch Center for Training and Sending (ACTS)
Kansas City, Missouri

7   Jim Elliot (1927-1956), *The Journals of Jim Elliot*, ed. Elisabeth Elliot, (Grand Rapids, MI: Revell, 1990), 72.

Preface

This book was written in memory of the martyrs of old, in honor of the martyrs at present, and for the preparation of the martyrs of the future. The following words of American missionary Samuel Zwemer—the "apostle to Islam"—serve as a fitting preface. The excerpt is taken from a chapter in a book published by the Student Volunteer Movement in 1911 entitled "The Glory of the Impossible."

> Great victory has never been possible without great sacrifice. If the winning of Port Arthur required human bullets, we cannot expect to carry the Port Arthurs and Gibraltars of the non-Christian world without loss of life.
>
> Does it really matter how many die or how much money we spend in opening closed doors, and in occupying the different fields, if we really believe that missions are warfare and that the King's Glory is at stake? War always means blood and treasure. Our only concern should be to keep the fight aggressive and to win victory regardless of cost or sacrifice. The unoccupied fields of the world must have their Calvary before they can have their Pentecost.

Raymond Lull, the first missionary to the Moslem world, expressed the same thought in medieval language when he wrote: "As a hungry man makes dispatch and takes large morsels on account of his great hunger, so Thy servant feels a great desire to die that he may glorify Thee. He hurries day and night to complete his work in order that he may give up his blood and his tears to be shed for Thee."[8]

May the Lord use this work to stir up another generation of martyr-missionaries, at home and abroad. Worthy is the Lamb.

Dalton Thomas
Tauranga, New Zealand
November 2011

---

8   Samuel Zwemer, *The Unoccupied Mission Fields of Africa and Asia*, (The Student Volunteer Movement; 1st Edition, 1911).

From prayer that asks that I may be
Sheltered from winds that beat on Thee,
From fearing when I should aspire
From faltering when I should climb higher,
From silken self, O Captain, free
Thy soldier who would follow Thee.

From subtle love of softening things,
From easy choices, weakenings,
(Not thus are spirits fortified,
Not this way went the Crucified)
From all that dims Thy Calvary
O Lamb of God, deliver me.

Give me the love that leads the way,
The faith that nothing can dismay,
The hope no disappointments tire,
The passion that will burn like fire;
Let me not sink to be a clod:
Make me Thy fuel, Flame of God.

—Amy Carmichael of Dohnavur[9]

9   Amy Carmichael, "Make Me Thy Fuel," *Mountain Breezes: The Collected Poems of Amy Carmichael,* (Ft. Washington: CLC Publications, 1999), 223.

Introduction
"He Has Been Enough"

The central premise of this book is that the call to martyrdom is foundational and indispensable to authentic apostolic Christianity.[1] When and where this calling is faithfully expounded, appropriately emphasized, and rightly demonstrated, the Church will mature and fulfill the high calling for which she was conceived. When and where it is avoided, omitted, dismissed, or rejected, the Church will exist beneath the intentions of God, in a state of general irrelevance before the peoples of the earth and the powers of the air.

This book was written in order to show that the biblical theology of martyrdom is the *normative call* to authentic Christianity. This theology is clearly evidenced in both the New Testament and Church history.[2]

1   By "apostolic Christianity," I mean "the sort of Christianity that the apostles embraced, taught, and demonstrated." In Jude 3 we are commanded to "contend earnestly for the faith that was delivered to the saints" at the start, to and through the apostles.

2   "Whoever does not bear his own cross and come after me cannot be my disciple." (Luke 14:27)

Though not every believer is called to give a martyr-witness, every believer is called to embrace a martyr-mentality, every Church a martyr-mandate, and every minister a martyr-theology. Whether we live or die is ultimately in the hands of our Master, and if we have not entrusted *Him* with that decision, we may be deluding ourselves into assuming we are His bondservants when in fact we are not.[3]

As long as we live under the influence of the assumption that *we* are not called to such a standard, we will, by default, live without "a proper and appropriate antagonism to the world in attempts to preclude the possibility that we might die the death of Christ. We [will then secure] our own fates as nonmartyrs."[4] Such self-preservation, however, does not befit those who worship a crucified King and a slain Lamb.

The Divisive Words of Jesus and the Devotion of the Weak

Throughout the three and a half years of His earthly ministry, Jesus consistently called His disciples to expect and embrace suffering, persecution, and martyrdom, exhorting them with such words as, "lose your life," "hate your life,"[5] "pick up your cross," and "deny yourself."[6] He assured us that we are "blessed" when we are "reviled" and "persecuted,"[7] and cursed if "all men speak well of us."[8] He regularly said things like, "Whoever does not bear his own cross and come after Me *cannot be*

---

3   Luke 14:27
4   Craig Hovey, *To Share in the Body: A Theology of Martyrdom for Today's Church,* (Grand Rapids, MI: Brazos Press, 2008), Kindle Edition, 18.
5   Luke 14:26
6   Mark 8:35-36
7   Matthew 5:10-12
8   Luke 6:26

My disciple"[9] and "A servant is not greater than his master. If they persecuted Me, they will also persecute you."[10] He made promises like, "You will have trouble,"[11] "they will put you to death,"[12] and "you will be hated by all for My name's sake."[13]

When the masses heard Jesus preaching such difficult and demanding words, they responded in very different ways. Some left everything they had in a moment and clung to Him. Others kept their distance. Some attempted to kill Him, and others ultimately did. It should come as no surprise then that, when those divisive words are proclaimed today, they elicit the same array of responses. Some find them liberating. Others find them offensive. Some embrace them. Others ignore them. Some receive them with joy. And others resist them in fear. But, most assuredly, when those holy words are faithfully echoed and courageously proclaimed, no man, woman, or child can remain indifferent.

My response to Jesus' call to "lose my life" is consistently changing. At times I find it enthralling. Other times I find it intimidating. Yet I have discovered that my experience is not unique. Such inconsistency is normal in the life of every believer. We are all on a journey of growing in the grace that empowers us to love Him more than that which He calls us to joyfully surrender. No one begins his or her journey fervent and mature. Like Solomon's Shulamite, we are constantly being tested and tried that our love for our Bridegroom would deepen.[14] Like Peter, we are being discipled by a Master who,

9   Luke 14:27
10   John 15:20
11   John 16:33
12   Matthew 24:9
13   Matthew 10:22
14   Jesus, John the Baptist, and the apostles referred to Jesus as a Bridegroom and to the climax of history as a wedding. See John 3:29:

as a skilled potter, molds us like clay until, over time, we are conformed to His image. My prayer is that this book would serve a generation who, like the Shulamite and Peter, desire dedication and devotion, but have discovered a divided heart in response to Jesus' difficult words. To such hungry souls, we would declare that He is worth more than anything we could ever gain, more precious than everything we could ever lose, and fully capable of shepherding weak and fearful hearts through the valley of the shadow of death.

He Has Been Enough

The fire of my convictions concerning the issue of martyrdom was kindled soon after my conversion. By studying its place in the New Testament, Church history, and biblical prophecy, those convictions have grown stronger with every passing year. But it wasn't until I read a statement by Amy Carmichael (1867-1951) that I felt I needed to commit my convictions to paper and openly beckon a generation to embrace them as their own.

Carmichael, after hearing Hudson Taylor speak in 1887 about the mandate concerning frontier missions, became convinced that the Lord was calling her to the nations and to a life of ministry. Before long, she left Ireland by ship as a single woman in her twenties bound for a distant and hostile land. She never returned. After spending over fifty-five years in Asia without furlough, she met her Maker face to face through a natural death at the age of eighty-three. She was buried in the Indian soil beneath a birdbath after requesting that no stone be set upon her grave.

Matthew 9:14-15; 22:1-2; 25:1-10; Ephesians 5:29-32; 2 Corinthians 11:1-3; Revelation 19:7; and 22:17.

Looking back over her life she penned the following:

> The night I sailed for China, March 3, 1893, my life, on the human side, was broken, and it never was mended again. *But He has been enough.*[15]

Few words have had as great an impact on my life as these. Like David Livingstone (1813-1873) before her who, after pouring his life out in Africa, said, "I never made a sacrifice,"[16] Carmichael bears witness to a precious and sublime truth: The call to martyrdom is not the exaltation of *death* as much as it is the exaltation of *Christ.* Martyrdom is the consummate expression of holy affection for the One we believe to be more precious than life and well worth the pain of death.

By saying, "He has been enough," she was saying, "It was all worth it." Or rather, "*He* was worth it." Through the decades of struggle, pain, loss, affliction, loneliness, toil, and trouble, she was convinced *He was enough.* In light of all that she left, all that she lost, all that she endured, she declared that she would do it all over again because it was all worth it. *He* was worth it. The Lord was more valuable to her than life and well worth all that she would lose in death. He was her everything. All her fountains were in Him.[17]

Though her life was "broken," her soul was satisfied. Christ was to her like "a treasure hidden in a field" for which she would "joyfully sell all to buy."[18] This is why, when asked by

---

15 Amy Carmichael, *A Chance to Die: The Life and Legacy of Amy Carmichael* by Elisabeth Elliott, (Grand Rapids, MI: Fleming H. Revell, 23rd printing, June 2003), 64.

16 Livingstone was a missionary to Africa. The quote was cited in Samuel Zwemer, "The Glory of the Impossible," *Perspectives on the World Christian Movement*, 3rd ed., Ralph D. Winter and Stephen C. Hawthorne, (Pasadena, Calif.: William Carey, 1999), 315.

17 Psalm 87:7

18 Matthew 13:44

a potential missionary candidate what it was like to be a missionary, Amy responded that missionary life was simply "a chance to die."[19]

Amy Wilson Carmichael did not give a martyr-witness in death. However, she did give one in life. Her joyful submission to the sovereign will of her Master, with no regard to the preservation of her own mortal flesh, expresses well the true spirit of the Gospel call: to give what we cannot keep to gain what we cannot lose.[20]

This is the center of the flame of the biblical theology of martyrdom: joyfully "counting everything as loss because of the surpassing worth of knowing Christ Jesus [our] Lord."[21] This alone can put the ultimate issue and holy call in its appropriate context.

Death is a means. Christ is the end. Joy is the motive. And glorious is the journey.

19 Amy Carmichael, *A Chance to Die: The Life and Legacy of Amy Carmichael* by Elisabeth Elliot, 176.
20 This is a paraphrase of the martyr Jim Elliot who said, "He is no fool who gives what he cannot keep to gain that which he cannot lose." [*Shadow of the Almighty: The Life and Testament of Jim Elliot* by Elizabeth Elliot, (1958), 108]. Though often attributed to Elliot, it is likely the quotation originated from Matthew Henry's biography of his father, English nonconformist clergyman Philip Henry (1631-1696), as "He is no fool who parts with that which he cannot keep, when he is sure to be recompensed with that which he cannot lose." [Matthew Henry, *The Life of the Rev. Philip Henry, A.M.*, Matthew Henry, ed. Sir J. B. Williams, (W. Ball, 1839), 35].
21 Philippians 3:7-8

CHAPTER ONE
MARTYRDOM AS A CONTINUUM

Our generation has witnessed its fair share of atrocities motivated by religious fanaticism and sectarian extremism. As a result, an exaltation of martyrdom such as this will undoubtedly be met with skepticism, scoffing, or scorn. Therefore, before we begin our study on this holy calling as it is set forth in Scripture, we must focus briefly on the continuum of martyrdom between the first and second comings of Jesus to observe how common it has been to the Church of Jesus Christ through history. A brief survey of martyrdom in the Church's past, present, and future will magnify the importance of this widely misunderstood and woefully neglected subject, and urge us to embrace it as an integral element of apostolic Christianity. Convinced that the persecution of the saints is central to the great Story of redemptive history, John Bunyan wrote that

A man when he suffereth for Christ, is set upon a *Hill*, upon a *Stage*, as in a *Theatre*, to play a part for God in the world.[1]

As we observe martyrdom's prominence throughout Church history, we are compelled to embrace this message as the normative call to true faith in Christ. Remembering those who have gone before us gives us considerable insight into how we are to relate to this issue in the present and in the future. Concerning the memorializing of martyrs, Craig Hovey writes,

> Martyrs are those who are remembered by the church for having carried crosses to death, thereby sharing in the death of Christ. By remembering them in this way, the church does not embrace death so much as embrace as part of its ongoing life those who have died in the cause of Christ. A martyr-church remembers its fallen members as followers of Jesus. Nevertheless, it is also appropriate that the church identify its martyrs as martyrs through a process of its life together. Whether its members are truly martyrs, and thus how they should be remembered, requires discernment.[2]

The memorializing of martyrs requires discernment because we must distinguish between the true and the counterfeit. Contesting the perverted pursuit of martyrdom in his day, Augustine wrote that

> They who seek the glory of the martyrs would rightly claim to be true martyrs if they had suffered for the right cause. The Lord did not say those who suffer will be blessed, but rather, those who suffer for the Son of Man, who is Jesus Christ.
>
> True martyrs are those of whom the Lord spoke, saying, "Blessed are they who suffer persecution for justice's sake." Therefore, not they who suffer for an iniquitous purpose, for the sinful destruction of Christian unity, but rather

---

1   Rev Jeremiah Chaplin, *The Riches of Bunyan*, (United Kingdom: Echo Library, 2007), 156.
2   Craig Hovey, *To Share in the Body: A Theology of Martyrdom for Today's Church*, 18.

those who suffer persecution for justice's sake, are to be ac-
counted true martyrs.[3]

MARTYRDOM AT THE BEGINNING

We begin our study by acknowledging the prominence of
martyrdom *at the beginning.* The early Church was birthed
and nurtured in a culture of martyrdom and was intimately
acquainted with Christ through the fellowship of suffering.
Church historian Stephen Neill wrote, "Every Christian [in
the first century] knew that sooner or later he might have to
testify to his faith at the cost of his life."[4] How could they not
in light of the martyrs that preceded them? In one concentrated timeframe, John the Baptist, Jesus, and Stephen were slain.
The bloody executions of these three men set a precedent for
first-century believers: In order to follow Christ, one must be
willing to die.

The prominent place of martyrdom in the early Church is
made evident by the stunning fact that in the wake of Stephen's
death (which was overseen by Saul of Tarsus, another future
martyr), nearly all of the original disciples were violently
killed. Church history suggests that of the twelve, it is possible
that only John the Beloved died a natural death. The blood of
all the others stained the far corners of the Roman Empire.

James, the son of Zebedee, was the first to know death as
gain when Herod Agrippa executed him with the sword in Jerusalem around AD 44.[5] Phillip was killed in Phrygia in AD 54
after his head was fastened to a pillar and rocks were hurled at
his defenseless body. In AD 63 James, the brother of Jesus, was

3   James E. Sherman, *The Nature of Martyrdom,* (Paterson, NJ: St. An-
    thony Guild Press, 1942), 61.
4   Stephen Neill, *A History of Christian Missions,* (Penguin, 1964), 43.
5   Acts 12:2

cast down from the Temple, stoned, and then beaten to death with a club. In AD 64 Barnabas was dragged out of the city Salamina on Cyprus and then burned. That same year Mark was dragged to the stake through the streets of Alexandria resulting in "his whole body [being] torn open, so that there was not a single spot on it, which did not bleed." He was dead before he reached the stake. Tradition suggests Peter was crucified upside down in Rome around AD 67-68. Andrew was crucified in Greece. Jude was killed in what is now Iran. And Thomas spilled his blood on the distant soil of India. The death of those young men[6] and the subsequent beheading of the apostle Paul marked the beginning of a historical continuum of martyrdom that persists to this very day. This leads us to the next point.

MARTYRDOM AT PRESENT

It is critical that we also acknowledge the prominence of martyrdom *at present*. Statistically speaking, the subject of martyrdom is more relevant now than it has ever been in light of the fact that it is now more prolific than it has ever been.

In the 2002 edition of the *Annual Statistical Table on Global Mission* David Barrett estimated that "approximately 164,000 Christians [would] die as martyrs [that year] and that the average number of Christian martyrs each year will grow to 210,000 by the year 2025."[7] According to Barrett's research, there were approximately 45,400,000 martyrs in the twentieth century.[8] This means that the previous century saw more

6   The details of the executions can be found in the first chapter of *The Martyrs Mirror* (VA: Herald Press, second reprint edition, 1938).

7   David Barrett, *Annual Statistical Table on Global Mission: 2002,* International Bulletin of Missionary Research 26, no. 1 (January 2002), 23.

8   David Barrett, George T. Kurian, and Todd M. Johnson, *World Christian Encyclopedia: A Comparative Survey of Churches and Religions— AD 30 to 2200,* vol. 1, (Oxford: Oxford University Press, 2001), 11.

martyrs than every century before it combined. In his book, *The New Persecuted* (*I Nuovi Perseguitati*), Italian journalist Antonio Socci argues that 65% of all Christian martyrs were slain in the twentieth century.[9]

In the time that it will take you to read this book, saints will be killed for their faith somewhere in the world. For believers in nations like Nigeria, Indonesia, Bangladesh, Iran, Columbia, and North Korea, the issue of martyrdom is a cold hard reality. To dismiss this subject is to dishonor those who at this very moment are faced with the threat of violence for their faith in Christ.

While we in the West may believe the subject of martyrdom to be fringe and irrelevant to our faith, the testimony of the slain around the world, *in our own generation*, urges us to reconsider. In view of the mounting violence against Christians in the nations, it is more likely that those who dismiss the issue of martyrdom are the ones whose beliefs are fringe and irrelevant, as statistics show that it is they who are the minority.

Martyrdom at the End

Finally, as we begin our study, it is imperative that we acknowledge the prominence of martyrdom *at the end* of the age.

The prophetic Scriptures are abundantly clear that the greatest expression of martyrdom will occur in the generation of the Lord's return after "the whole world" receives a "witness" concerning "the Gospel of the Kingdom."[10] The penetration of the Gospel into every nation, tribe, and tongue will result in a bloody backlash. This is not to say that the end-time missions thrust will

9   "Twentieth Century Saw 65% of Christian Martyrs," *EWTN* (website), Accessed November 2011, http://www.ewtn.com/vnews/getstory. asp?number=26402.

10   Matthew 24:14

be unfruitful. On the contrary, men, women, and children from every nation will vow their allegiance to Jesus. The final push towards global evangelism will be met with vehement rage. Jesus said that as the Gospel of the Kingdom is being heralded across the Earth during the tumultuous time of tribulation, "all nations will hate" believers and "put [them] to death."[11] The impact of this unprecedented wave of persecution will claim the lives of Christ-followers in "every nation, people, tribe, and tongue."[12] This is a staggering prophetic reality. *Every nation* will be painted red with the blood of the faithful. These end-time martyrs will "come up out of the great tribulation" to be counted among the "full number" of martyrs which, according to Jesus, has already been ordained in God's sovereignty.[13]

The prophetic texts speak of an age-ending scourge in which a satanic tyrant will be granted authority "to make war on the saints and to conquer them."[14] Christians will be "given into his hands" and will be "worn out" as he "makes war with them" and "prevails over them."[15] During that final time of "tribulation," that tyrannical "man of sin"[16] will "destroy mighty men and the saints"[17] as he "goes out with great fury to destroy and devote many to destruction."[18] Many in that day will "stumble by sword and flame, captivity and plunder."[19]

Martyrdom will be so prolific in that final hour that Jesus declared it to be one of the premier signs of the times indicating

11   Matthew 24:9-14
12   Revelation 7:9-14
13   Revelation 6:9-11
14   Revelation 13:7
15   Daniel 7:21-25
16   "Man of sin" is the title Paul gave this man commonly referred to as "the antichrist" or "the beast."
17   Daniel 8:24
18   Daniel 11:44
19   Daniel 11:33-34

the nearness of His return and the end of the age.[20] If we ignore or dismiss this issue now, we seal our fate as those who will be unprepared to "stand" and "endure" in the midst of the coming storm.

A Word to Christians in the Western World

The prominence of martyrdom at the beginning of Church history, the prominence of martyrdom at present, and the prominence of martyrdom at the end of the age all urge us to acknowledge it as a valid historical continuum as well as a prophetic reality for which we should prepare. But despite the fact that martyrdom has been a present and abiding experience for Christians in much of the Earth since the stoning of Stephen, many will struggle to accept these realities because they have never personally known persecution. Because of the measure of safety they now enjoy and because of the time and place in which they now live, many find it difficult to embrace the call to martyrdom on the grounds that their environment does not require them to. But dismissing or avoiding the issue on these grounds alone is foolish. The call to martyrdom is standard for every believer regardless of when or where they live. Articulating the way in which we should approach the subject of martyrdom, Hovey writes

> I do not accept that it falls only to others to reflect on the meaning of martyrdom as a New Testament assumption and mandate. Instead, I take seriously [the] responsibility I believe to be incumbent on all Christians, including those in first-world comfort: to refuse to relegate the threat of martyrdom to the fringes of history or remote parts of the globe. The church may well discover that some settings are more hostile than others, that the world exhibits more and

20 Matthew 24:3-14

less hospitality to Christ's heralds depending on the mode of its witness, the whims of rulers, and a multitude of other factors. But it is my conviction that the periods and places of quiet are exceptions to the rule and more often reflect the church's willingness to accommodate to its host culture than indicate that culture's inherent goodness.[21]

As we begin this study on the call to martyrdom, I would encourage you to carry the testimony of the faithful witnesses of the past, present, and future close to your heart. Their deaths give profound meaning to our lives and make much of the One we love so dearly. But as important as the testament of history is, it is not the primary reason we should embrace the call to martyrdom. It is first and foremost the Holy Scriptures that bid us "come and die."

MARTYRDOM AS INTRINSIC TO THE APOSTOLIC GOSPEL

Martyrdom is so prominent in history because martyrdom is so central and intrinsic to the Gospel. From the start, it was the normative call to discipleship for all who would follow Christ.

A disciple is not above his teacher, nor a servant above his master. It is enough for the disciple to be like his teacher, and the servant like his master. If they have called the master of the house Beelzebul, how much more will they malign those of his household. (Matthew 10:24-25)

If sinful men killed our Teacher and Master, what reason do we have to not expect the same treatment? Are we "above" Him in this regard? Or are we to anticipate a shared experience of suffering? Is this not the ultimate paradigm of Christian obedience?

21 Craig Hovey, *To Share in the Body: A Theology of Martyrdom for Today's Church*, 14-15.

The Gospel is defined in the New Testament in terms of Jesus' sacrifice *for us* and *never* in terms of our sacrifice *for Him.* But it must be acknowledged that the New Testament stresses that those who wish to bind themselves to the crucified Lord must first "lose their lives" in order to do so. Dietrich Bonhoeffer was right in saying that, "The only man who has the right to say that he is justified by grace alone is the man who has left all to follow Christ."[22]

The crosses we bear and the deaths we die can never save us. Christ's cross and Christ's death alone are the only grounds of our salvation. But we must never emphasize this truth in such a way that diminishes Jesus' insistence upon self-denial and cross-bearing for those who wish to follow Him. After prophesying of His own death by crucifixion, He turned to the disciples and called them to theirs.[23] The call to "pick up your cross," "deny yourself," and "lose your life," is at the center of Jesus' preaching and teaching. It is inseparable from the message of "Christ and Him crucified."[24] His cross makes sense of ours, and our cross makes much of His. Martyrdom "is an aspect of the gospel in the world, an intrinsic quality of the cross of Christ, and therefore a mark of the church both in how it remembers those who have died and in how it prepares and trains its members for faithfulness."[25]

The issue of martyrdom was powerfully brought to bear upon the conscience of the American Church in 1956 when Jim Elliot, Nate Saint, Ed McCully, Roger Youderian, and Pete Fleming were slain in the jungles of Ecuador. In the preface

22 Dietrich Bonhoeffer, *The Cost of Discipleship,* (New York: Macmillan, 1967), 55.
23 Mark 8:35-36
24 1 Corinthians 1:18-2:5
25 Craig Hovey, *To Share in the Body: A Theology of Martyrdom for Today's Church,* 19.

of *Shadow of the Almighty: The Life and Testament of Jim Elliot*, (first published in 1958), Elisabeth Elliot wrote of the death of her husband and his friends saying,

> Jim's aim was to know God. His course, obedience–the only course that could lead to the fulfillment of his aim. His end was what some would call an extraordinary death, although in facing death he had quietly pointed out that many have died because of obedience to God. He and the other men with whom he died were hailed as heroes, 'martyrs.' I do not approve. Nor would they have approved.
>
> Is the distinction between living for Christ and dying for him, after all, so great? Is not the second the logical conclusion of the first? Furthermore, to live for God is to die, 'daily,' as the apostle Paul put it. It is to lose everything that we may gain Christ. It is in thus laying down our lives that we find them.
>
> Those who want to know [Christ] must walk the same path with him. These are the 'martyrs' in the scriptural sense of the word, which means simply 'witnesses.' In life, as well as in death, we are called to be 'witnesses' – to 'bear the stamp of Christ.'
>
> I believe that Jim Elliot was one of these. His letters and journals are the tangible ground for my belief. They are not mine to withhold. They are a part of the human story, the story of a man in his relations to the Almighty. They are facts."

The call to martyrdom is the call to know Christ, to follow Christ, and to bear witness about Him to the nations. This has been the case since the first century and will continue until the end.

CHAPTER TWO
MARTYRDOM AS JOY

The word "martyr" comes from the Greek word μάρτυς, which our English Bibles translate as "witness." For example, in Acts 1:8 we read, "you will be my *witnesses* in Jerusalem and in all Judea and Samaria, and to the end of the earth." At the time when the New Testament was written, "martyr" simply meant, "witness." Nowadays, however, dictionaries define the word in terms of "the suffering of death according to one's faith." Martyrs are those who choose allegiance to Christ over life when the luxury of enjoying both is denied.[1]

---

1   In his book about Raymund Lull, the fourteenth-century martyr-missionary to Muslims, Samuel Zwemer wrote: "It was the teaching of the medieval Church that there are three kinds of martyrdom: The first both in will and in deed, which is the highest; the second, in will but not in deed; the third in deed but not in will. St. Stephen and the whole army of those who were martyred by fire or sword for their testimony are examples of the first kind of martyrdom. St. John the Evangelist and others like him who died in exile or old age as witnesses to the truth but without violence, are examples of the second kind. The Holy Innocents, slain by Herod, are an example of the third kind." (Samuel M Zwemer, *Raymund Lull: First Missionary to the Moslems,* [Diggory Press, 2008] Kindle Edition.)

TO LIVE IS CHRIST

While martyrdom is preeminently a mode of dying, it m
also be considered a mode of living. Of this we must be sure
There is no true death for Christ that is not the fruit of a true
life for Christ. That is, no one has ever died for the Lord who
had not first lived for Him. This is why Paul could say, "For me
to live is Christ, and to die is gain."[2]

The supremacy of Christ over all things in life and in death
is the theological foundation to the call to martyrdom. One
cannot say, "Death is gain," until he can say, "Christ is life."
And one cannot say, "Christ is life," apart from the thought of
"death as gain." To avoid one at the expense of the other is to
disfigure the Gospel. They stand or fall together.

When we walk in the conviction that Christ is more valuable than life, and well worth the momentary sting of death,
we have come to embrace the true spirit of martyrdom. The
mandate to "lose our lives"[3] by "not loving them unto death"[4]
rests entirely on the foundational biblical command to "de-
light in the Lord."[5] The event of martyrdom *as death*, therefore, is the consummate and ultimate expression of our joy in
God *in life*.

Therefore, embracing the call to martyrdom is not so much
about aiming to *die well* as much as it is about aiming to *love
well*. However, it just so happens that the more our love for
Jesus matures in strength and fervor, the more our love for our
lives will diminish. As the Lord in His grace brings us forth
into such love,[6] we will find ourselves longing for Him with

2   Philippians 1:21
3   Mark 8:34-36
4   Revelation 12:11
5   Psalm 37:4
6   John 17:24-26

such ardent desire that we will be compelled to say with Paul, "Which shall I choose [between life and death]? I cannot tell. I am hard pressed between the two."[7] This is the language of a martyr's love.

Steve Saint, the son of martyr-missionary Nate Saint, explained what motivated his father saying,

> Dad strove to find out what life really is. He found identity, purpose, and fulfillment in being obedient to God's call. He tried it, tested it, and committed himself to it. I know that the risk that he took, which resulted in his death and consequently his separation from his family, he took not to satisfy his own need for adventure or fame, but in obedience to what he believed was God's directive to him. I suppose he is best known because he died for his faith, but the legacy he left his children was his willingness first to live for his faith.[8]

Nate Saint found what life really is—"To live is *Christ*." The result of this discovery was that he lived as though death was gain.

TO DIE IS GAIN

Until we consider death to be gain, we will be living beneath the intentions of God. This is why Paul declared that his highest ambition was to "know Him and the power of His resurrection, [sharing] in His sufferings, becoming like Him in His death."[9] Love for Christ that is unwilling to suffer and allegiance to Him

---

7   Philippians 1:22-23
8   The excerpt comes from a highly recommended essay written by Steve Saint that was included in the book *Martyrs: Contemporary Writers on Modern Lives of Faith* compiled by Susan Bergman, (Maryknoll, NY: Harper San Francisco, 1996), 142-154.
9   Philippians 3:10

that is not "unto death," are wanting of apostolic character.[10] Such love and allegiance cannot be conjured up in the flesh. They are the fruit of the work of grace; they are the overflow of a satisfied soul. Therefore, the call to "suffer" and "die" is first and foremost a call to encounter the One who causes us to see death as gain and suffering as incomparable to the weight of glory that is ours in Him.

Addressing the relationship between suffering and joy in the life of the believer, John Piper explains that

> we measure the worth of a hidden treasure by what we will gladly sell to buy it. If we will sell all, then we measure the worth as supreme. If we will not, what we have is treasured more. "The kingdom of heaven is like treasure hidden in a field, which a man found and covered up. Then in his joy he goes and sells all that he has and buys that field" (Matt. 13:44). The extent of his sacrifice and the depth of his joy display the worth he puts on the treasure of God. Loss and suffering, joyfully accepted for the kingdom of God, show the supremacy of God's worth more clearly in the world than all worship and prayer.[11]

With a wealth of experience behind him, J. Hudson Taylor (1832-1905), the famous pioneer missionary to China, declared the same message.

> It is in the path of obedience and self-denying service that God reveals Himself most intimately to His children. When it costs most we find the greatest joy. We find the darkest hour the brightest and the greatest loss the highest gain. While the sorrow is short-lived and will soon pass away, the joy is far more exceeding…it is eternal.[12]

10 "…through many tribulations we must enter the kingdom of God." (Acts 14:22)
11 John Piper, *Let the Nations Be Glad!*, (Grand Rapids, MI: Baker Book Group, 2010), Kindle Edition, 93.
12 Hudson Taylor, *China's Millions*, (London: Morgan & Scott, 1884), 102.

THE PARADOX OF MARTYRDOM

Martyrdom is a paradox. It is the ultimate loss. And it is the ultimate gain. Yet it is only because the worth of that which we gain far exceeds the value of that which we lose, that we can face it with joy. Herein lies the true spirit of martyrdom. It is the consummate expression of the joy of the saints in Christ.

Paul prefaced his declaration of death as gain by explaining that his greatest ambition was to "honor" Christ "by life or by death." In other words, the issue was not the superiority of life over death or death over life, but rather, the superiority of Christ over everything. This is why Paul would also say that all the things he would "gain" in life and all the things that he would "lose" in death were insignificant in light of the magnificent worth of Christ.

Until we are individually and collectively convinced that Christ is more precious than "life" and well worth the pain of "death,"[13] we have yet to know Him as we ought. Until we are persuaded with the host of the slain that the cause of Christ's fame among the nations is worth the investment of our life-blood—should it be required of us—we have yet to know Him as we must. Until our anthem has become, "To live is Christ, to die is gain,"[14] we have yet to know Him as He wishes to be known—as "a treasure in a field" and "a pearl of great price" that we would be wise to "joyfully sell all we have to buy."[15] Until the Church's witness among the nations emanates this ancient and apostolic glory through the cracks of earthen vessels such as you and me, we can and must be sure that we have yet to give the witness that we were called to give.

13 Philippians 3:7-11
14 Philippians 1:21
15 Matthew 13:44-45

Individuals who are free from the fearful avoidance of death are a threat to the powers and principalities of the air and are an agitation to sinful men who hate the One to whom their joy bears witness. Thus we mustn't emphasize martyrdom as a mode of living to the effect that it undermines martyrdom as a mode of actually dying. When the disciples heard Jesus call them to follow Him by denying themselves, picking up their crosses, and losing their lives, they did not receive it as a metaphor. Within a few decades almost every one of them was executed for their allegiance to the Lamb. And it was not because they sought death, but because their joy—and their treasure—was in Christ.

SUFFERING PERSECUTION WITH JOY

G. K. Chesterton once said that Jesus promised His disciples three things: that they would be completely fearless, absurdly happy, and constantly in trouble.[16] In the midst of profound suffering, the early Church possessed deep and authentic joy. For example, read Luke's record of how the early Church responded to persecution.

> When they had called in the apostles, *they beat them* and charged them not to speak in the name of Jesus, and let them go. Then they left the presence of the council, *rejoicing that they were counted worthy to suffer dishonor for the name.* (Acts 5:40-41)

Note in verse 41 the juxtaposition of the words "rejoicing" and "suffer." Not only were they glad *in the midst of their suffering*, they were glad *because of their suffering*. Like Christ Himself

---

16 William Barclay, *The Gospel of Luke*, (Louisville, KY: Westminster John Knox Press, 2001), 92.

who "for the *joy* set before Him"[17] endured the violent and unjust treatment from the hands of wicked men, the first generation of Christians embraced the crucible of affliction with gladness. They counted it a privilege to suffer with Him because they knew that they would, therefore, reign with Him.[18] This is why the apostles spoke about persecution and suffering as a privilege, a gift, and an honor that is "granted" to us by the Lord.[19] Before being crucified upside down, the apostle Peter wrote the following to a community bearing the onslaught of persecution for their faith.

> Beloved, do not be surprised at the fiery trial when it comes upon you to test you, as though something strange were happening to you. But rejoice insofar as you share Christ's sufferings, that you may also rejoice and be glad when his glory is revealed. If you are insulted for the name of Christ, you are blessed, because the Spirit of glory and of God rests upon you. But let none of you suffer as a murderer or a thief or an evildoer or as a meddler. Yet if anyone suffers as a Christian, let him not be ashamed, but let him glorify God in that name. (1 Peter 4:12-16)

In verse 12 he speaks of suffering as a "fiery trial" of which we should "not be surprised" "as though" it were an anomaly that God is impotent to deliver us from. He argues that suffering is to be anticipated, expected, and embraced by the Christian as normal and even inevitable. Then in verse 13 he contrasts the word "surprise" with "rejoice," saying that, when we bear unjust treatment at the hands of sinful men, we are "sharing Christ's sufferings." It is this sharing, in Peter's mind, which is counted as an honor. At the core of Peter's theology of suffering was the issue of our "rejoicing," "gladness," and

17 Hebrews 12:2
18 2 Timothy 2:8-13; Romans 8:17
19 Philippians 1:29

"blessedness." And so it should be central to the theology of martyrdom.

A DEEP AND EXTRAORDINARY ECSTASY

Believers in the first century are not the only ones who "rejoiced" with "gladness" in the face of suffering. Christians throughout Church history have experienced the same joy in the midst of the cauldron of affliction because of the Spirit-wrought revelation of the worth of Christ with whom the slain will reign. To tell every one of their stories would fill libraries. One testimony in particular has had an incalculable impact since it was penned.

While Richard Wurmbrand died a natural death at the age of ninety-two in California in 2001, he is no less a man "of whom the world is not worthy"[20] on account of his suffering for the Gospel. Wurmbrand, a Romanian minister, was brutally tortured after planting underground Churches and openly challenging the Communist regime in the 1940s. He was arrested in 1948 and endured fourteen years of imprisonment for his faith (two separate terms), three of which were spent in solitary confinement in a twelve-by-twelve-foot cell without windows or lights.[21] In the preface to his book *God's Underground,* he wrote the following as he remembered his incarceration:

> The prison years did not seem too long for me, for I discovered, alone in my cell, that beyond belief and love there is a delight in God: a deep and extraordinary ecstasy of happiness that is like nothing in this world. And when I came out

20 Hebrews 11:38
21 I highly recommend Richard Wurmbrand's book, *Tortured For Christ,* (Bartlesville, OK: Living Sacrifice Book Company).

of jail I was like someone who comes down from a mountaintop where he has seen for miles around the peace and beauty of the countryside, and now returns to the plain.[22]

Wurmbrand's testimony, as with Carmichael's before him, gives me courage to believe what Paul said about "these light and momentary afflictions" being altogether "incomparable" to the "weight of glory" of gaining Christ in the end.[23] It was "for the joy set before"[24] Him that Jesus faithfully entrusted His spirit into the hands of His Father and embraced His call to death. And it is for the joy set before us that we can do the same.

22 Richard Wurmbrand, *In God's Underground*, (Portland, OR: Living Sacrifice Book Company, 2011), Kindle Edition.
23 2 Corinthians 4:17
24 Hebrews 12:2

Chapter Three
Martyrdom As Love

Having defined the call to martyrdom as the consummate expression of a believer's joy in Christ, let us now turn our attention to the issue of love: the supreme virtue, the highest calling, and the principle motive of all true Christ-exalting loss and death.

Since the commandment to "love the Lord" is the "greatest"[1] of them all, it is imperative that it shapes our understanding of the call to martyrdom. According to Paul, love, along with joy, is at the core of this critical theology.

Only a lovesick heart can say with joy, "To live is Christ, to die is gain," and really mean it. To the man or woman whose heart is mighty in love, death does not intimidate. Death is only a threat to our deepest joy when Christ is not the object of our deepest love. But when our love for Him exceeds our love for life, our joy is invincible, both in life and in death. In his book *Tortured for Christ*, Richard Wurmbrand wrote that,

1   Matthew 22:37-39

if the heart is cleansed by the love of Jesus Christ, and if the heart loves Him, one can resist all tortures. What would a loving bride not do for a loving bridegroom? What would a loving mother not do for her child? If you love Christ as Mary did, who had Christ as a baby in her arms, if you love Jesus as a bride loves her bridegroom, then you can resist such tortures . . . God will judge us not according to how much we endured, but how much we could love. The Christians who suffered for their faith in prisons could love. I am a witness that they could love God and men.[2]

Wurmbrand goes on to testify,

It was in prison that we found the hope of salvation for the Communists. It was there that we developed a sense of responsibility toward them. It was in being tortured by them that we learned to love them.[3]

While it is true that "he who *endures* to the end shall be saved,"[4] the human heart cannot endure suffering for Christ's name's sake apart from the sustaining power of love. We could rightly say then, "He who *loves* to the end shall be saved." For endurance is impossible without it.

Distinguishing the Holy from the Profane

The proliferation of Islamic jihad through the heinous atrocity of suicide terrorism has made the issue of martyrdom one of the great social, religious, and geo-political crises of our time. It is essential, therefore, that we are able to distinguish between the holy and the profane with regard to death for God.

---

2   Richard Wurmbrand, *Tortured For Christ*, (Bartlesville, OK: Living Sacrifice Book Company), Kindle Edition, ch. 2.

3   *Ibid.*

4   Matthew 24:9-14

To those who are bondservants of Jesus, martyrdom is the act of *giving* our lives in love for the sake of *salvation*, not the *taking* of lives in rage for the sake of *destruction*. We believe that the principle motive behind Christ-rejecting Islamic martyrdom is corrupt. We believe that such violence is sinister and altogether devoid of virtue. Therefore, we soberly maintain that the ultimate and inescapable end of such brutality is eternal punishment and everlasting shame. We heartily reject Islamic martyrdom as well as any and all forms of martyrdom that seek to take the lives of others through violence. Piper rightly identifies the "fundamental difference" between the New Testament call to "lose our lives" and that within Islam saying,

> First, the life of a Christian martyr is taken by those whom he wants to save. He does not fall on his own sword, and he does not use it against his adversary. Second, Christian martyrs do not pursue death; they pursue love. Christians do not advance the cause of the gospel of Christ by the use of the sword: "For all who take the sword will perish by the sword" (Matt. 26:52). Jesus said, "My kingdom is not of this world. If my kingdom were of this world, my servants would have been fighting. . . . But my kingdom is not from the world" (John 18:36). Christianity advances not by shedding the blood of others, even if it is mingled with ours.[5]

At this juncture it behooves us to acknowledge that a defiled spirit of martyrdom is not unique to Islam. According to the New Testament, it is well within the realm of possibility for our embrace of the call to martyrdom, and even the sacrifice itself, to be devoid of God-honoring virtue—a reality that Peter found out the hard way. The passage that makes this the clearest is 1 Corinthians 13.

5 John Piper, *Let the Nations Be Glad!*, 97.

IF I HAVE NOT LOVE

In 1 Corinthians 13:3 the apostle Paul (who himself ultimately gave a martyr-witness) spoke of martyrdom saying, "If I give away all I have, and if I deliver up my body to be burned, but have not love, *I gain nothing.*" The implications of this statement are staggering.

Paul emphasizes the loss of material possessions through generosity ("if I give away all that I have") and the loss of mortal life through martyrdom ("if I deliver my body to be burned"). Then he explains that it neither honors the Lord nor benefits the slain if the sacrifice is not motivated by love. Martyrdom then, in its purest essence, must be defined as an outward expression of an internal reality of affection.

Acts of sacrifice, in themselves, bear no inherent virtue. So it is with martyrdom, the ultimate sacrifice. It is the motive from which the act derives that determines whether or not Christ is pleased and the martyr profited.[6] This means that the embrace of the call to martyrdom could be as offensive to the Lord as the rejection of it if the outward expression is motivated by the same inward corruption. If our sacrifice does not spring from the overflow of love, then it is of no value, and we will "gain *nothing,*" even if we give *everything.* It is not the giving of the sacrifice that matters, but rather the hidden motive of the heart that gives rise to it.

The last stanza of Isaac Watts's classic hymn *When I Survey the Wondrous Cross*[7] poignantly articulates the true spirit of martyrdom.

---

6   In Matthew 16 and Mark 8 Jesus appealed to the disciples to embrace self-denial and death on the basis that it would profit them.

7   The original title of this hymn was "Crucifixion to the World by the Cross of Christ."

Watts wrote:

> Were the whole realm of nature mine,
> That were an offering far too small.
> Love so amazing, so divine
> Demands my soul, my life, my all.

This puts the issue of sacrifice into perspective. If everything in the whole realm of nature belonged to us, we would not be considered foolish in the end if we were to count it loss for the sake of gaining Christ. Some would consider such extravagance wasteful and offensive in light of all the glory and riches contained within the universe. But to those who love the Lamb—He who has loved us with such an "amazing" love—the offering of such glory and riches is paltry and contemptible. An episode in the Gospels sheds considerable light on the wisdom of extravagant sacrifice for the sake of love.

A BEAUTIFUL WASTE

Before making the descent into Jerusalem for the Passover, at which time He was to be killed, Jesus stopped in Bethany—one of the few places in Israel where our Lord could rest and be Himself among friends.

One evening at dinner, exactly a week before the crucifixion,[8] a young woman named Mary approached Jesus as He was reclining. In her hand was a jar full of costly oil. Though the flask was small, it contained oil (or perfume) that was equivalent in value to a full year's worth of wages.[9] Compelled by an overwhelming sense of necessity, she opened her vial and poured it upon Jesus' head and feet before "wiping

8   John 12:1-6
9   In John 12:5 Judas says that it is worth 300 denarii. This was at that time equivalent to one year of wages.

41

[them] with her hair." As she did, "the house filled with the fragrance of the perfume."[10]

Here, in one holy moment, this young woman liquidated what would have been the modern day equivalent of $40,000 (USD). Such a lavish expression of devotion was the fruit of her conviction that the value of her costly oil was eclipsed by that of the God-Man before whom she stood.

As soon as the oil was poured forth, the atmosphere in the room shifted as tensions began to mount. A few individuals rushed to end what they believed to be an awkward and embarrassing episode. Judas, the traitor who later sold Jesus to the authorities for thirty shekels, was first to lift his voice in protest, publicly declaring the foolishness of her act. Seeking to humiliate the young woman, he informed those in the room that her oil was worth a year of wages and could have been much better spent on ministry endeavors. Moved by his apparent compassion for the poor, the other disciples began glaring at her with the same scornful eyes (it's sobering that the soon-to-be leaders of the Church were so easily swayed by such a deceiver). As fragrance from the oil filled the home, tempers began to flare. Matthew recorded it this way:

> And when the disciples saw it, they were indignant, saying, "*Why this waste*? For this could have been sold for a large sum and given to the poor." (Matthew 26:8-9)

Those in the room saw her display of devotion as excessive, unnecessary, and foolish. The thought of it made them furious.

Imagine the scene. Her family standing aloof, horrified at what she had just done; Judas standing over her with pointed finger and open disdain, and the rest of the disciples murmuring their self-righteous objections as they awaited Christ's

10   John 12:3

response. Through it all, Mary sat trembling. With tears of love yet dripping from her face, and the oil of devotion from her hair, her heart beat with the fear of uncertainty. For how could she know the manner in which Jesus would respond? Would He look upon her offering with the same contempt as the rest in the room? Or would He be honored by it?

Her heart was soon settled as Jesus publicly and tenderly affirmed her sacrifice, saying,

> Why do you trouble the woman? For *she has done a beautiful thing to me. . .* For in pouring this fragrant oil on my body, *she did it for my burial.* Assuredly I say to you, wherever this Gospel is preached in the whole world, *what this woman has done will also be told as a memorial to her.* (Matthew 26:10-13)

Mary of Bethany was overwhelmed with loving devotion. And it resulted in the spontaneous liquidation of her financial stability for the years to come. Whatever 300 denarii meant to her, Jesus meant more. Whatever position she enjoyed because of it, she enjoyed the position that Jesus secured for her more. Whatever this inheritance was to her, Jesus was more.

Jesus was deeply moved by what she had done. So as to silence her critics and comfort her fearful heart, He spoke. He affirmed that what she had done was "beautiful." It was wise. It was virtuous. And it was pure. He declared that what she had done was the fruit of her revelation of His imminent death. Her extravagance was in response to His extravagance. Knowing that He would soon pour out His blood from holy veins, Mary felt that nothing was more fitting in that moment than to pour out that costly oil from her vial. Finally, He said what she had done was to be forever memorialized by being told in all the nations where the Gospel is taken. Jesus wanted the disciples to remember this moment forever. Moreover, He wanted all the nations to remember it forever.

Friends, I ask you: Is the inheritance that is yours in Christ of greater value than your earthly everything? Oh, for the grace to love Him with such abandon! Will you pour out at His feet that which you hold as most precious? Will you give yourself fully unto Him and care not when the world scorns, "Look how he is just throwing away his life," or "What a waste of her time and energy." **Let us** persist through the earthly shame and lay it all down for a greater heavenly reward.

MARTYRDOM AS THE FRAGRANCE OF EXTRAVAGANT DEVOTION

While she never gave a martyr-witness in death (that we know of at least), Mary of Bethany exemplifies the martyr-spirit more clearly than anyone in the New Testament (which is why Jesus commanded the disciples to tell her story to every people and nation to which they would be sent). The fragrance of her devotion prophesied of the sacrifice of those future martyrs present in the room that night. Through those young men, "the aroma of Christ" would be diffused[11] among the nations in which they would later bleed.

The disciples would never forget the scent of that perfume. The memory of its fragrance and the devotion it represented remained with them until the day that they poured out their own vials in the same holy passion that gripped this precious woman from Bethany.

Mary poured out her oil. The disciples poured out their blood. And in the eyes of the Lord, both offerings were

11   2 Corinthians 2:14-17

beautiful, not simply because they were costly, but because they were motivated by love. *This* is the true spirit of martyrdom.

Chapter Four
Martyrdom as Grace

Inasmuch as martyrdom is an expression of our joy *in* God and the overflow of our love *for* God, it is furthermore a gift *from* God. The sacrifice of martyrdom is a gift of grace.

True, Christ-exalting martyrdom is not born of the world, the flesh, or the devil. It is a phenomenon wrought by the Spirit. It is for this reason that Paul was so emphatic in his declaration that suffering for the name of Jesus, especially when it is unto death, is a "work" of God in the hearts of His people. To the Philippians who were being buffeted by persecution, he wrote,

> And I am sure of this, that he who began *a good work in you* will bring it to completion at the day of Jesus Christ. It is right for me to feel this way about you all, because I hold you in my heart, for *you are all partakers with me of grace, both in my imprisonment and in the defense and confirmation of the gospel.* (Philippians 1:6-7)

The evidence of the "work" of God "in" the Philippians

was in their suffering of mistreatment for their embrace and "defense" of "the Gospel." This "grace" of which they were all "partaking" was a *grace to bear with* reproach and abuse with patience, gentleness, and profound joy. Later he reiterates this in more explicit terms saying that,

> *it has been granted to you* that for the sake of Christ you should not only believe in him *but also suffer* for his sake. (Philippians 1:29)

Suffering—like the gift of faith—is "granted" by God. This includes martyrdom. It is imperative that we understand that martyrdom is never to be conjured up. It is not to be forced or induced in the flesh, and is never to be sought. Suffering is to be received and celebrated, like the persecution that fell upon the disciples of the early Church who "went away rejoicing [when] they were counted worthy to suffer dishonor for the name."[1]

When Jesus called His disciples to "pick up" their "crosses" and "lose their lives," He was not asking them to seek death through a carnal determination to bleed. He was calling them, rather, to submit their lives into His hands and allow Him to write their stories. It was His prerogative alone as to whether or not they would die a martyr's death. Thus the early Church viewed their suffering, persecution, and martyrdom as gifts received by grace.

THE TRANSFORMATION OF SIMON PETER

One of the clearest biblical examples of martyrdom as a gift of grace is in the life of Simon Peter.

It is generally accepted by Church historians that Peter

---

1   Acts 5:41

was executed in Rome, having been crucified upside down. Around AD 80-98, Clement of Rome wrote,

> Through envy and jealousy, the greatest and most righteous pillars [of the Church] have been persecuted and put to death. Let us set before our eyes the illustrious apostles. Peter, through unrighteous envy, endured not one or two, but numerous labours, and when he had finally suffered martyrdom, departed to the place of glory due to him.[2]

Against the expectations of Satan and undoubtedly many of the disciples, Peter paid the ultimate price and suffered the ultimate loss in martyrdom. The cowardly man who denied Jesus three times on the eve of the crucifixion was forged by grace and emboldened by the Spirit to remain faithful in his devotion to Jesus, even unto death. Simon Peter's transformation from a sinful fisherman to an apostle and martyr of the Lamb ended in violence, as his life was brutally taken from him.

It is a joy to celebrate the triumph of grace at the end of his story, as he died like his Master. But Peter didn't begin his story in the same state of fervency and faithfulness that we see at the end. Quite the opposite, Peter's martyrdom was the fruit of a long journey in grace that prepared him for that consummate sacrifice.

The Scriptures record in vivid detail the conflict within Peter as Jesus beckoned him to "lose his life." Peter's response to this call was as inconsistent as ours is (which makes his testimony so relevant). In this chapter we will trace Peter through the Gospels, taking note of his various responses to the call to suffering and death throughout. We will see him rejecting it,

2 Clement, "Letter to the Corinthians" (Chapter 5), *Early Christian Writings* (website), accessed November 2011, http://www.earlychristian-writings.com/text/1clement-roberts.html.

embracing it, perverting it, desiring it, despising it, and everything in between. And in his stumbling, the issue of martyrdom as grace shines like the sun in all its splendor.

It benefits us, then, to take a closer look at Peter's life and to consider how radically different his responses were when confronted with the issue of martyrdom. These episodes give us profound insight into the true spirit of martyrdom, mostly by seeing its counterfeit in Peter's blunders and the ultimate triumph of grace in the end.

The Initial Call to Martyrdom—Matthew 16

The first time Peter grappled with the issue of martyrdom was in Matthew 16 after Jesus spoke of His own execution. Before Jesus made His descent into Jerusalem to be crucified, He gathered the disciples and said plainly to them that He would "be killed and on the third day raised."[3] He emphasized this event as the chief reason for which He was sent. Upon hearing this Peter cringed and recoiled. Matthew records that he then

> took him aside and began to rebuke him, saying, "Far be it from you, Lord! This shall never happen to you." (Matthew 16:22)

The thought of Jesus' bleeding, suffering, and dying was too much to bear. He had never considered a battered and defeated Messiah. To Peter's carnal mind, it was an offense. His response? Here, in one of the greatest displays of human arrogance in history, Simon Peter takes the Lord of Glory aside and rebukes Him. He didn't question Him or express confusion. Peter rebuked Him. Attempting to take charge of the situation before it spiraled out of control, Peter belted out, "This

3   Matthew 16:21

shall *never* happen to you," so as to say, "Not now, not tomorrow, not next week, not *ever*." Matthew records what happened next.

> But he turned and said to Peter, "Get behind me, Satan! You are a hindrance to me. For you are not setting your mind on the things of God, but on the things of man." (Matthew 16:23)

Jesus' response to Peter was three-fold. First, He addressed Satan as the source of Peter's passion. Second, He declared that Peter was a hindrance to Him, that he was an obstruction to His sovereign purposes. And third, he said that Peter's convictions were born of the flesh, like all fallen men. It would be difficult to exaggerate how devastating and humiliating this would have been for Peter to be cut down by his Rabbi before his peers.

Jesus discerned that there was more to Peter's antagonism than just the threat of losing a best friend. Jesus understood that this episode of Peter's arrogance was the bitter fruit of a deep-rooted system of offense related to the issue of suffering and death. Instead of lopping off the fruit of Peter's stupidity and moving on, Jesus then turned to His disciples and sought to tear up the root, saying,

> If anyone would come after me, let him deny himself and take up his cross and follow me. For whoever would save his life will lose it, but whoever loses his life for my sake will find it. For what will it profit a man if he gains the whole world and forfeits his life? Or what shall a man give in return for his life? (Matthew 16:24-26)

This is the first open call to martyrdom in the Gospels. While Jesus called His disciples to bear suffering, persecution, and reproach many times before, this is the first time Jesus asks them to lay down their lives in the same way that He was about to lay His life down. Jesus was charging them to embrace solidarity with Him in His sufferings. But take note of the way Jesus articulated that call. Suffering and death was not an end, but a means. The central statement in this passage is "follow Me." If we ever exalt the call to "take up a cross" over the call to "follow Jesus," we have misrepresented our Lord and His words. Jesus placed the primary emphasis on following Him and not on death. He was asking them to seek Him, not suicide. Yet in His omniscience, He knew that this would result in death for nearly all of them. Their deaths were not the fruit of seeking martyrdom but of following Christ. Hovey rightly says that

> it is not possible to become a martyr by directly seeking it or in some way killing oneself. Martyrdom is different from suicide. Seeking martyrdom is succumbing to the temptation to separate "take up your cross" from "follow me."[4]

This foundational call to self-denial, crucifixion, and loss of life was a defining moment in Peter's life. Until this point, Peter had no paradigm for suffering, crucifixion, or martyrdom. The very mention of it was an offense to his carnal triumphalism. In many ways, particularly in relation to understanding and embracing Christ's call to martyrdom, this is where Peter's journey began. Likewise, it is where *our* journey begins. None of us finds the call to death attractive on the front end. We find it deeply offensive. Often, like Peter, we too are so convinced of the wisdom and theological accuracy of our convictions that we feel no shame in boldly rejecting it to Jesus' face. I believe we all may have been guilty of this at one time or another.

4   Hovey, *To Share in the Body: A Theology of Martyrdom for Today's Church*, 50-51.

We would do well, as Peter did, to begin our journey with the painful realization that our minds are filled with the thoughts of man and not the thoughts of God. If not repented of, this mindset causes us to be a "hindrance" to Jesus and a danger to ourselves.

THE UPPER ROOM—MATTHEW 26 AND JOHN 13

On the eve of Jesus' crucifixion, He gathered His disciples and sought to inform them of what was about to happen. His words that evening had a profound impact on Peter. Matthew 26 and John 13 record the exchange.

> "Little children, yet a little while I am with you. You will seek me, and just as I said to the Jews, so now I also say to you, 'Where I am going you cannot come.' A new commandment I give to you, that you love one another: just as I have loved you, you also are to love one another. By this all people will know that you are my disciples, if you have love for one another." Simon Peter said to him, "Lord, where are you going?" Jesus answered him, "Where I am going you cannot follow me now, but you will follow afterward." Peter said to Him, "Lord, why can I not follow you now? I will lay down my life for you." Jesus answered, "Will you lay down your life for me? Truly, truly, I say to you, the rooster will not crow till you have denied me three times." (John 13:33-38)

Peter answered Him, "Though they all fall away because of You, I will never fall away." Jesus said to him, "Truly, I tell you, this very night, before the rooster crows, you will deny me three times." Peter said to Him, "Even if I must die with You, I will not deny You!" And all the disciples said the same. (Matthew 26:33-35)

Compare the language that Peter uses in these two passages with the language Jesus used in Matthew 16. In Matthew 16

Jesus said, "*Follow* Me," and "Lose your *life*." Then, in John 13, after saying, "Where I am going you cannot come," Peter says, "Why can I not *follow* You?" and "I will lay down my *life* for You." Matthew records that Peter said, "Even if I must *die* with You, I will not deny You!"

Peter's declarations in John 13 and Matthew 26 are his attempts to embrace what Jesus called him to in Matthew 16. While Peter was convinced of the nobility of his loyalty to his Master, Jesus discerned that something was amiss in the heart of His friend. Instead of honoring Peter's vow of allegiance, the Lord took advantage of the situation to humble him before his peers saying, "You will deny Me three times."

This interaction in the Upper Room is profoundly relevant to our consideration of the call to martyrdom. In Matthew 16 Peter rejects the call to death. In Matthew 26 and John 13 he embraces it. But in each episode Jesus rebukes him. Both Peter's rejection and embrace of the call to bear a cross and die were offensive to Jesus.

Peter's consent to die with Jesus in the Upper Room represents the second stage we are each required to walk through in the journey of losing our lives for His sake. Initially, we all, like Peter, respond with offense and rejection to the call (as in Matthew 16). Yet even when we eventually embrace it, as Peter did, we do in such a way that offends the Lord through pride, elitism, competitiveness, and arrogance (as in Matthew 26).

We can take heart that both stages are necessary and to some degree unavoidable. No one whom Jesus calls begins his or her journey as a mature follower. We all begin as poor followers of a Great Leader who will never leave us or forsake us, even when we, like Peter, swing from one illegitimate extreme to the other.

THE GARDEN—JOHN 18, MATTHEW 26, AND LUKE 22

Peter's defiled spirit of martyrdom reaches its fullest expression hours later in the Garden of Gethsemane when Judas arrives with guards to take Jesus. John 18, Matthew 26, and Luke 22 describe it from different perspectives.

> Then Simon Peter, having a sword, drew it and struck the high priest's servant and cut off his right ear. (The servant's name was Malchus.) So Jesus said to Peter, "Put your sword into its sheath; shall I not drink the cup that the Father has given me?" (John 18:10-11)

In the face of violence, Peter exerted force to avert it. Because he didn't understand the purpose of Jesus' death and could not perceive the necessity of His suffering, Peter sought to avoid the situation altogether by physical aggression. However, at the very same time, Peter was acting out his sincere but unsanctified desire to die with Jesus. As he drew his sword against the guard, presumably in an attempt to strike at his neck, Peter was putting his life on the line. The problem, however, was this was not the sort of death that Jesus called him to. The death to which Christ had called Peter was a death of humble submission to persecutors who would unjustly inflict violence against him for his allegiance to Jesus. Sadly, Peter did not yet understand this, and apparently, neither did the other disciples.

> And when those who were around him saw what would follow, they said, "Lord, shall we strike with the sword?" And one of them struck the servant of the high priest and cut off his right ear. But Jesus said, "No more of this!" And he touched his ear and healed him. (Luke 22:49-51)

The true spirit of martyrdom is displayed through the stark

contrast of the disciples' willingness to "strike with the sword" and Jesus' willing surrender to his enemies. The display became all the more radiant as Jesus reached out to touch *and heal* the wound of His adversary before being hauled to trial. By rebuking Peter and healing the guard, Jesus publicly declared His disapproval of the spiteful blow dealt by His cowardly protégé.

This episode sheds glorious light on the theology of God-glorifying martyrdom. Jesus' rebukes of Peter and the disciples show us what He was *not* looking for. And the loving touch of the guard whom Peter struck was a tender example of what He *was* looking for.

The Denials—John 18

Shortly after Jesus healed the guard, rebuked Peter, and was carried away by the guards, Peter was again confronted with the issue of martyrdom. As Jesus was taken into the court of the high priest, Peter stood outside awaiting news of what was to come of this tragic night. There he was approached by a servant girl in charge of guarding the door to the court and later a relative of the man he attacked. This was the setting for Peter's famous three-fold denial of his Lord. Asked whether he was a follower of Jesus and the man who drew his sword in the garden, Peter responded, "I am not." The third time he said it, a rooster crowed just as Jesus prophesied. This began the darkest seventy-two hours Peter had ever known.

The Beach—John 21

In Matthew 16 Peter rejects the call to martyrdom. In John 13 he embraces it in a sinful way. In Luke 22 he expresses his rejection of the call and the defiled spirit with which he embraced it in the Upper Room. Finally, in John 18 he retreats in cowardice and publicly denies Jesus three times.

However, the story comes to its redeeming climax in John 21 where Jesus appears on the beach at dawn and calls out to Peter, Thomas, Nathaniel, James, and John who had all decided to return to fishing in the wake of the death of their Rabbi.

It is difficult to imagine Peter's mental agony at this point in the story. It could be argued that the other disciples had faithfully stood by their Lord until the end. Yet Peter had denied Him not once, but three times, and had therefore broken fellowship with Christ. Some commentators suggest that it was in confusion, despondency, and humiliation that Peter retreated to his previous occupation, perhaps sensing his own lack of worth to a higher calling.

In one of the most precious episodes in the Gospels, Jesus reenacts the scenario in which He first met Peter and called him to follow Him. When Jesus *first* approached Peter on the beach in Luke 5, it was after a long night of fishing with no success. Here, in Luke 21, the Lord approaches Peter again under the same circumstances—another long night with no fish to show for it. In both passages, Jesus charges the men to throw their nets on the right side of the boat. Formerly, in Luke 5, the bulging nets break. Yet here in John 21, we are told that "though there were so many [fish], the nets were not torn" (v. 11).

This second time on the beach, Simon Peter's response to the resurrected Lord is deeply moving. Where only a few chapters before we read of him shrinking back, distancing himself, and denying Christ, here, we see the same heart-sick man leaping into the water, longing desperately to close the distance separating him from his Lord. Jesus was, in essence, starting over with Peter. He was giving him the chance to lay down his life again. Yes, Peter had stumbled, but not so as to fall, and Jesus refused to let this be the end of the story. Here, as "dawn began to break" (v. 4), announcing a new day after a barren night, Jesus would tenderly prove that His mercies are indeed "new every morning," and His faithfulness "great."[5] Looking into Peter's shame-filled eyes Jesus quietly asked,

> "Simon, son of John, do you love me more than these?" He said to him, "Yes, Lord; you know that I love you." He said to him, "Feed my lambs." He said to him a second time, "Simon, son of John, do you love me?" He said to him, "Yes, Lord; you know that I love you." He said to him, "Tend My sheep." He said to him the third time, "Simon, son of John, do you love me?" Peter was grieved because he said to him the third time, "Do you love me?" and he said to him, "Lord, you know everything; you know that I love you." Jesus said to him, "Feed my sheep. Truly, truly, I say to you, when you were young, you used to dress yourself and walk wherever you wanted, but when you are old, you will stretch out your hands, and another will dress you and carry you where you do not want to go." (This he said to show by what kind of death he was to glorify God.) And after saying this he said to him, "Follow me." (John 21:15-19)

At the end of the story of Peter's transformation, with fellowship restored, we find Jesus prophesying to Peter about his future execution. After charging him to embrace the call to leadership with the command to "Feed My lambs," "Tend My sheep," and "Feed My sheep," Jesus charged him once more to embrace the call to martyrdom. He revealed that Peter's hands would be "stretched out" as he was "dressed" and "carried where he would not want to go." He would pour out his lifeblood as an offering to the kindest Man he had ever known. This offering, he was told, would greatly "glorify God."

5   Lamentations 3:22-23

ARM YOURSELVES WITH THIS SAME WAY OF THINKING

Peter's journey began with a fervent resistance to the idea of crucifixion. And it ended in a God-glorifying execution. God's purpose ran its course. Grace had triumphed. And Christ was honored in Peter's life and death.

Each of the different stages of Peter's growth in the grace of martyrdom is important for us to consider and understand, as they represent the very same stages of growth that we too must pass through. Peter's journey sheds light on the ways in which redeemed but immature followers of Jesus respond to His commands to lose our lives for His name's sake. If we are ignorant of these truths we too may find ourselves being rebuked by Jesus for agreeing with Satan, exercising violent force, or retreating in cowardice and apostasy when confronted with the threat of death for our allegiance to our Master.

In the face of persecution, the Church is forced to reject the call to martyrdom, defile it, or embrace it. To embrace it requires an understanding of suffering in God's purposes and a renewing of our mind according to the Word of God. After being transformed himself, it was Peter who called others to the same, saying,

> Since therefore Christ suffered in the flesh, *arm yourselves with the same way of thinking.* (1 Peter 4:1)

Clearly, this exhortation came from a man who had finally "gotten it"—from one who had resisted and wrestled, struggled and stumbled, but who, in the end, surrendered and embraced this transformational mindset. For Peter, the issue of suffering was the issue of grace. It was a work of the Holy Spirit in the life of a weak and broken man. Consider the literal translation of the following words from 1 Peter 2:19-20.

> *This therefore is grace*: if for the sake of conscience toward God a man bears up under sorrows when suffering unjustly. For what glory is there if, when you sin and are harshly treated, you endure it with patience? But if, when you do what is right and suffer, you patiently endure it, *this is grace before God*.[6]

Brothers and sisters, let us also determine together to "arm *ourselves* with the same way of thinking" that Jesus demonstrated through His submission to suffering and death according to the will of God. *This* is the standard to which we are called—*this* is the path we are asked to walk. Surely we too can embrace this commission, being confident that the way is made by grace alone, through faith alone, in Christ alone, and to the glory of God alone.

With our lives and in our deaths, may we seek to worship Him who *alone* is worthy of all.

---

6   Josef Ton, *Suffering, Martyrdom, and Rewards in Heaven*, (Wheaton, IL: The Romanian Missionary Society, 1997), 258-259.

CHAPTER FIVE
MARTYRDOM AND MISSIONS

Inasmuch as the call to martyrdom is integral to the Gospel, it is likewise indispensable to the task of global missions. The theology of martyrdom is not just a personal discipleship issue; it is a Great Commission issue. As Christ-followers, we must faithfully and consistently speak of it as such, especially with regard to the daunting task of global evangelization in an increasingly hostile season of history. The "blood of the martyrs is seed"[1] that must be sown in the field of the nations before salvation springs up from the ground.

The advance of the Gospel among the unreached peoples of the Earth has always been costly. History shows that the proverbial roots of the Church grow the best in soil that has been saturated with the life-blood of missionaries. These are those who have counted Christ and His fame among the nations as

---

1   This famous statement comes from the fiftieth chapter of Tertullian's classic work, *Apologeticus*, that was published in AD 197. A translation of the statement in context is, "The oftener we are mown down by you, the more in number we grow; the blood of Christians is seed."

more precious than the preservation of their own lives. Are we so foolish as to believe that such a price will not be required of us in our own generation—one in which over *six thousand people groups* have still yet to hear the Gospel?

In the same way that Jesus' resurrection was preceded by His death and burial, so also must Gospel victory among the nations be preceded by the sacrifice of selfless bond-servants. In John 12 Jesus made this clear by declaring that His death was to be a model and an example for those who would follow and serve Him.

> And Jesus answered them, "The hour has come for the Son of Man to be glorified. Truly, truly, I say to you, *unless a grain of wheat falls into the earth and dies, it remains alone; but if it dies, it bears much fruit.* Whoever loves his life loses it, and whoever hates his life in this world will keep it for eternal life. *If anyone serves me, he must follow me; and where I am, there will my servant be also.* If anyone serves me, the Father will honor him. (John 12:23-26)

Unless *missionaries* fall to the earth and die, they will remain alone; but if they die, they will bear much fruit. It was true of Jesus, the greatest missionary of all. And according to Him, it is true for all who serve and follow Him into the ripe harvest fields of the unreached and unengaged.

THE GOSPEL OF THE KINGDOM AND THE END OF THE AGE

Many leading missiologists believe that, despite the fact that there are over six thousand unreached people groups on the planet, it is not only possible for them to be reached within our children's lifetime,[2] some are even saying that it is *likely*

2   "Although many people are still unreached, the number is only a fraction of that of 100 years ago. *The goal is attainable in our generation. . ."* (Patrick Johnstone, *The Church Is Bigger Than You Think,* [Ross-shire,

that they will be. This is exciting, but this is also sobering for a number of reasons.

First, Jesus said that when "the Gospel of the Kingdom [is] proclaimed throughout the *whole world* as a testimony to *all nations . . .* then the end will come."[3] This means that global missions and the consummation of this age are inextricably bound together in God's sovereign purposes. If we are on the brink of seeing all nations receive a witness, then we are also on the threshold of the end of this age and the inauguration of the next.

Second, it means that our generation has been entrusted with the sublime privilege of engaging the nations and people groups that have been avoided or forgotten for the last two thousand years of Church history. Friend, they have been avoided or forgotten for a reason. To remember them and relate to them requires a martyr-mentality.

The Difference Between Domestic Ministry and Frontier Missions

The call to martyrdom is not reserved exclusively for those saints living in hostile nations who face the threat of violence for their faith in Jesus. It is something that *every believer* is called to embrace. However, without minimizing or negating that reality, let us now consider the importance of embracing a martyr-mentality within *frontier missions* specifically. To do so, it is essential to first distinguish between domestic ministry and frontier missions.

In the New Testament there is a clear distinction between the work of the evangelist in a location where the Gospel has

UK: Christian Focus, 1998], 105–107.)

3   Matthew 24:14

penetrated at some level, and a location where the name of Jesus has never been spoken. A comparison of two passages makes this distinction quite clear. In 2 Timothy, we read Paul's words to a young man who was established in a city (possibly Ephesus) where Paul had previously labored.[4] He wrote to Timothy saying,

> Do the work of an evangelist, fulfill your ministry. (2 Timothy 4:5)

The "work of an evangelist" and the "ministry" to which Timothy was called was in a city in which the Gospel had already been preached and a Church already established. This is what we mean by "domestic ministry." He was laboring in a location in which the Gospel had already penetrated. He was hard at work among a community in which seeds of Gospel truth were being scattered by an established Church body. Let's compare this with Romans 15 where Paul explains his own calling.

> I make it my ambition to preach the gospel, not where Christ has already been named, lest I build on someone else's foundation. (Romans 15:20)

Timothy was fulfilling a ministry of *domestic* evangelism. Paul was fulfilling a ministry of *frontier* evangelism. Timothy was "building on a foundation" that was laid by "another." Paul was driven by passion to lay the foundation in regions where there wasn't one.

EMBRACING THE CALL TO FRONTIER MISSIONS

Frontier missions and domestic evangelism are both legitimate callings that are indispensable to the advance of God's

4   See Acts 19

purposes in the nations. It is important therefore that we do not exalt one above the other. Both are to be honored, proclaimed, and embraced. Some are called to pour themselves out in "Ephesus" where the Gospel has taken root, and some are called to pour themselves out in "Macedonia" where the name of the Lord has yet to roll from the tongue of even one individual. We must be careful to never hold one in a higher regard than the other. However, with that said, it is apparent that the Church needs to hold frontier missions in a higher regard *than we currently do*. Tragically, at this point, frontier missions is simply not a priority to most in the Western Church. We invest less than 1% of our resources into ministry to unreached people groups. This means that either God is unconcerned about the issue (which leaves *Him* responsible for the near wholesale avoidance of these people), or it is we who are indifferent (which places the guilt of negligence upon *us*). The website of one missions organization puts it this way:

> If everyone is obeying God's "calling" to be a missionary wherever they are then God is calling 99.9995% of people to work among the 44.3% of the world population that already has the gospel, and calling virtually no one (.0005%) to relocate among the other 53.7% of the world population that are not Christian. You have a better chance of being in a plane crash than being one of the 2 billion Christians in the world that are UPG [Unreached People Groups] missionaries.[5]

The fact that we in the West are so unconcerned about the unreached and unengaged is an injustice of epic proportions. Still, after two thousand years, half of the Earth's population has never met an ambassador for Christ! In the book *The Spiritual*

5   *The Traveling Team* (website), accessed October 2011, http://www. thetravelingteam.org/node /186/generalstatistics.

Secret of Hudson Taylor, the son and daughter-in-law of the frontier missionary recall the story of an interaction between Taylor and a new and deeply grateful Chinese convert. The new believer confronted him and

> unexpectedly raised the question: "How long have you had the Glad Tidings in your country?" "Some hundreds of years," was the reluctant reply [from Taylor]. "What! Hundreds of years? My father sought the Truth," he continued sadly, "and died without finding it. *Oh, why did you not come sooner?*" It was a moment, the pain of which Hudson Taylor could never forget, and which deepened his earnestness in seeking to bring Christ to those who might still be reached.[6]

FREE FROM THE FEAR OF DEATH

The question posed to Taylor stands as an indictment of the Church in our generation, and as a challenge to every believer. *Why* have so few gone? *Why* are there still so many unreached peoples? *Why* are there no laborers in so many fields that are ripe for harvest? The answer to these questions is simple: fear. Fear of loss, fear of pain, fear of death. To embrace the call to frontier missions, we must first be freed from the bondage of fear. One of the ways God delivers His laborers from such oppression is through the testimony of those who have gone before us and found Christ to be more valuable than life and worth the momentary pain of death. Among that company of martyr-missionaries is John G. Paton (1824-1907).

Paton was a Scottish missionary to Vanuatu (Pacific islands known then as The New Hebrides). He paid an immeasurable

6   Dr. and Mrs. Howard Taylor, *Hudson Taylor's Spiritual Secret,* (Chicago, IL: Moody Publishers, 1955), 81.

price embracing the mandate of frontier missions. He buried five children and his first wife on the field and saw very little fruit from his costly ministry. Through it all, the revelation of the worth of Christ sustained him, compassion for the un-reached motivated him, and the reality of martyrdom inspired him. Though he died from natural causes at the age of eighty-two, Paton deserves to be counted among the slain. He was a dead man walking.

Prior to the arrival of the Paton family, John Williams and James Harris from the London Missionary Society landed on the shores of Vanuatu in November of 1839. They were the first and only Christians to have ever stepped foot on the islands. Their ministry was short-lived. Within minutes of arriving on the island of Erromanga, both were brutally killed and eaten by cannibals. Forty-eight years later, John Paton took this as reason to follow in their footsteps saying,

> the New Hebrides [were] baptized with the blood of martyrs; and Christ thereby told the whole Christian world that He claimed these islands as His own.[7]

Paton was not deterred by the death of the missionaries. He was inspired and emboldened. He knew that their bloodshed would guarantee a harvest of souls for Christ. And so he went to reap.

THE NOBLEST SERVICE OF ALL

The end of Paton's ministry is as moving as the beginning. Looking back on the years of labor among the cannibals of Vanuatu he wrote:

---

7   John G. Paton: *Missionary to the New Hebredes, An Autobiography Edited by His Brother*, (Edinburgh: The Banner of Truth Trust, 1965, orig. 1889, 1891), 75.

Let me record my immovable conviction that this is the noblest service in which any human being, can spend or be spent; and that, if God gave me back my life to be lived over again, I would without one quiver of hesitation lay it on the altar to Christ, that He might use it as before in similar ministries of love, especially amongst those who have never yet heard the Name of Jesus. Nothing that has been endured, and nothing that can now befall me, makes me tremble – on the contrary, I deeply rejoice – when I breathe the prayer that it may please the blessed Lord to turn the hearts of all my children to the Mission Field and that He may open up their way and make it their pride and joy to live and die in carrying Jesus and His Gospel into the heart of the Heathen World![8]

Oh that God would raise up a generation of young missionaries who are free from the fear of death! The harvest is still plentiful and the laborers are still few!

Ed McCully's Desire

Scores of missionaries in the latter half of the past century found courage to embrace the call to the frontier after the slaying of the "Ecuador Five." In a letter dated 22 September 1950, almost six years before his death, Ed McCully wrote to Jim Elliot explaining how God had called him to lay his life down among the unreached.

Since taking this job things have happened. I've been spending my free time studying the Word. Each night the Lord seemed to get hold of me a little more. Night before last I was reading in Nehemiah. I finished the book, and read it through again. Here was a man who left everything as far as position was concerned to go do a job nobody else could handle. And because he went the whole remnant back in Jerusalem got right with the Lord. Obstacles and hindrances

8   *Ibid*, 444.

fell away and a great work was done. Jim, I couldn't get away from it. The Lord was dealing with me. On the way home yesterday morning I took a long walk and came to a decision which I know is of the Lord. In all honesty before the Lord I say that no one or nothing beyond Himself and the Word has any bearing upon what I've decided to do. I have one desire now—to live a life of reckless abandon for the Lord, putting all my energy into it.

Maybe He'll send me someplace where the name of Jesus Christ is unknown. Jim, I'm taking the Lord at His Word, and I'm trusting Him to prove His Word. It's kind of like putting all your eggs in one basket, but we've already put our trust in Him for salvation, so why not do it as far as our life is concerned? If there's nothing to this business of eternal life we might as well lose everything in one crack and throw our present life away without life hereafter. But if there is something to it, then everything else the Lord says must hold true likewise. Pray for me, Jim.[9]

Among those who were stirred to missions by the martyrdom of Ed McCully and his comrades was David Sitton. David has invested most of his adult life into the task of reaching the tribal people of Papua New Guinea with the Gospel. In his book *Reckless Abandon* (inspired by the letter above), he writes of how the Lord called him into frontier ministry. His perspective on "risk" is profound.

Here is my rationale for regularly sending missionaries with the gospel into hostile surroundings: Risk assumes the possibility of loss and is always determined by the value of the mission. The gospel is so valuable that no risk is unreasonable. Life is gained by laying it down for the gospel. If I live, I win and get to keep on preaching Christ. If I die, I win bigger by going directly to be with Christ and I get to take a few tribes with me.

9   David Sitton, *Reckless Abandon,* (Greenville SC: Ambassador International, 2011), Kindle Edition, Introduction.

I conclude that "losing my life" for the gospel is literally impossible because my years on this earth are worth far less than the value of the eternal gospel. . . If this is true, there is no meaningful risk for me as a carrier of the gospel of Christ. If some tribal chief chops my head off, he's doing me a favor. Think about it. If I get to (not have to) lay down my life in some remote jungle swamp, but God uses my death as an object lesson to turn their eyes to Christ and His name and the gospel gets established among an unreached people group somewhere, that isn't a bad "risk" for me. I didn't lose; I won! It was the bargain of a lifetime because Jesus is worth a lot more than my little life.

If we, as gospel ambassadors, are unwilling to suffer even as much as soldiers and firemen, could the reason be that we don't treasure Christ enough or value the gospel enough to sacrifice significantly for its advancement into unreached regions? Is Jesus simply not worth the risk to many of us? Where is the line over which it is no longer worth it to go with the gospel?[10]

INVESTING OUR EVERYTHING FOR THE SAKE OF CHRIST'S FAME AMONG THE NATIONS

For those who desire to contribute to the completion of what the apostles began in Jerusalem two thousand years ago, the theology of martyrdom is essential. It was essential at the beginning, and it will be essential at the end. It is the standard to which we as missionaries are called, and it is the standard by which we must call others. If the issue of martyrdom is not emphasized, the Church in the nations will be unprepared for the pressures associated with the Great Commission. The enterprise of world evangelization will require the investment of everything we have—even our blood.

Appealing to the Western Church to embrace the risk of

10   *Ibid.*

martyrdom for the sake of frontier missions, Dr. Michael L. Brown tells the story of an Indian evangelist who considered death as gain.

> In 1984, after hearing K. P. Yohannan of Gospel for Asia preach a challenging message, a Christian man named Samuel gave up his good job in South India and moved with his family to the region of Karnataka. There he began preaching to unreached Hindus, known for their hostility to the gospel. The Lord blessed the work, and even a Hindu priest was born again.
>
> This was more than the extremists could take. They burst into a meeting one Sunday and severely beat Samuel with iron rods, breaking his hand, arm, leg, and collar bone. When his seven year old son ran up and cried out, "Please don't kill our daddy!" they struck the boy on the spine, breaking his back. Then they left, warning Samuel that if he ever preached there again, they would kill him. The beating was so severe that Samuel and his son were hospitalized for several months.
>
> After his release, Samuel attended a workers' meeting with K. P. Yohannan. The first night, during a time of prayer, his arm was supernaturally healed of paralysis he was suffering as a result of his beating. The next night he testified of the things he had recently experienced for the Lord.
>
> K. P. asked Samuel, "What are you going to do now?" With a peaceful determination, the young man replied:
>
> "I am going back. Even if I am killed, my blood will be the foundation for many more churches."
>
> He returned and has continued to preach. His son is back in school and is also doing well. And Samuel has baptized many more converts — and has been beaten again.[11]

---

11 Michael L. Brown, "The Gospel of Martyrdom vs. the Gospel of Success," *Voice of Revolution* (website), accessed November 2011; http://www.voiceofrevolution.com/2008/12/13/the-gospel-of-martyr-dom-vs-the-gospel-of-success/

The crucified Christ is most faithfully represented in the world through a crucified Church. We are called to "fill up what is lacking in the sufferings of Christ."[12] Christ bled to redeem men out of every tribe and tongue. And though He cannot suffer in front of them personally and visibly as He did atop Golgotha, we can. When we do, we can be certain that His worth is displayed and His cross is magnified more powerfully than by any other means.[13]

CONCLUSION

Our proclamation of "the Gospel of the Kingdom to the whole world"[14] will be undermined to the degree that our desire to preserve our lives rivals our desire to "finish [our] course and the ministry that [we] received from the Lord Jesus, to testify to the gospel of the grace of God."[15] Or, to say it positively, our contribution to the task of global missions will be as great as our conviction that the fame of Christ's name

12 Colossians 1:24
13 Commenting on Colossians 1:24, John Piper writes, "Paul's sufferings fill up Christ's not by adding anything to their worth, but by extending them to the people they were meant to bless. What is lacking in the afflictions of Christ is not that they are deficient in worth or merit, as though they could not sufficiently cover the sins of all who believe. What is lacking is that the infinite value of Christ's afflictions are not known in the world. They are still a mystery (hidden) to most peoples. And God's intention is that the mystery be revealed, extended to all the Gentiles. So the afflictions are lacking in the sense that they are not seen and known among the nations. They must be carried by ministers of the Word. And those ministers of the Word fill up what is lacking in the afflictions of Christ by extending them to others." ("Called to Suffer and Rejoice: To Finish the Aim of Christ's Afflictions," Desiring God [website], accessed December 2011; http://www.desiringgod.org/resource-library/sermons/called-to-suffer-and-rejoice-to-finish-the-aim-of-christs-afflictions)
14 Matthew 24:9-14
15 Acts 20:24

among those who are perishing is worth the investment of our mortal lives. Without that conviction, we simply will not go.

Chapter Six
Martyrdom and Islam

The Joshua Project[1] has done extensive research concerning the progress of the Gospel in the nations among the unreached and unengaged. Their research puts the task of frontier missions in perspective.[2] As of November 2011, they reported the following statistics about the progress of the Gospel by people group and global population.

Progress by People Group
Total People Groups: 16,750
Unreached People Groups 6,921
% People Groups Unreached: 41.3 %

Progress by Population
World Population: 6.83 Billion
Population in Unreached People Groups: 2.84 Billion
% of Population in Unreached People Groups: 41.5%

1   Visit joshuaproject.net for more information.
2   Statistics of this kind vary depending on who is compiling the information and how. The Joshua Project is the most reliable by virtue of their extensive research.

The largest religious block on the map of the unreached and unengaged is Islam. The Joshua Project reports these sobering statistics.

- The population of the Muslim world is 1,537,185,000.
- Within that population of 1.5+ billion people are 2,840 different unreached *people groups*.
- 87.4 % of those 1.5+ billion people have yet to hear the Gospel.
- Or, to say it another way, 1,343,613,000 Muslims have yet to hear the name of Jesus.

While every religious block constitutes a substantial challenge to the global Church, clearly Islam is the most daunting. It is the largest as well as the most hostile. Consequently, the number of missionaries on the field is tragically few.

Joshua is the Executive Director of i2 Ministries. He trains students and missionaries globally in Christian Apologetics to Islam. In the wake of the September eleven attacks, he explained the level of missional activity within this block by saying that

Only one percent of all Christian missionaries go to do direct ministry amongst Muslims (1,800 missionaries total). That's one missionary for every 550,000 Muslims! For every Mormon you have ever met, there are 130 Muslims in the world. That's equivalent to having about five churches and 150 pastors for all of North America. Said differently, it would be like having the option to go to church in Texas (if you're fortunate to be that close) or say Boston perhaps, and three other locations in the U.S. on any given Sunday morning.[3]

3   Joshua Lingel, "Consider Again Your Vocation," *i2 Ministries* (website), accessed November 2011, http://www.i2ministries.org/index.php?option=com_content&view=article&id=13:consider-again-your-vocation&catid=27:articles-category&Itemid=72.

This should take our breath away, *especially* considering that the challenge of engaging the Islamic world is not new. Writing from Bahrain in 1902, Samuel Zwemer, the American missionary, historian, and "apostle to Islam," appealed to an emerging generation of Christians saying that

> the twentieth century is to be preeminently a century of missions to Moslems.[4]

The twentieth century has come and gone. And the majority of the Islamic world remains unreached and unengaged. While the number of laborers has considerably increased since Zwemer's day, so also has the population of Muslims. In other words, we are no closer now than we were one hundred years ago to accomplishing the task of establishing a faithful Gospel witness among those whose allegiance now belongs to Mohammed. The proverbial boundaries of the field have expanded, and the Church in the West has not proportionally expanded *her* efforts to reap it. Thus, it is a harvest which remains ready, yet largely unengaged.

THE FINAL FRONTIER OF GLOBAL MISSIONS: ISLAM

The challenge of serving the Muslim world demands a thoughtful and sober response. This will be the final frontier of world missions and the Church's greatest challenge. It will by no means be the *only* challenge. But it will be the greatest, and the costliest.

The Church is long overdue in her response to embrace the responsibility of engaging the Islamic world. The *dangers* that will accompany our doing so are real. But so are the

4   Samuel M. Zwemer, *Raymund Lull: First Missionary to the Moslems,* (Diggory Press, 2008) Kindle Edition, Preface.

scriptural *commands* to preach the Gospel to all peoples, and the *promises* of a harvest from every tribe and tongue. The moment we exalt the dangers above the commands and the promises that accompany them, we have gone astray. Thus, while it would be foolish to ignore the dangers, we must be careful to view them in light of all that Jesus has commanded and promised us.

The way in which we, as Christ's ambassadors, will enter such hostile regions of the globe today is by laying down our rights and expectations of coming out of them alive. This is not to say that we should go seeking after martyrdom, but rather that we relinquish our prerogative to avoid it at all costs. The dangers associated with the task of evangelizing the Islamic world are real. We must understand them, and by God's grace, face them. The price of laboring to set Christ above Mohammed, and the crescent beneath the cross, will surely be imprisonment and martyrdom for many. Yet in order for the twenty-first century to be different than the last, we must be willing to pay such a price.

The question that the Church must ask, then, is whether or not such an endeavor is worth the cost. Judging by the fact that these nations receive so few missionaries tells us that most of the Church would say that it is not. But Paul would say that it is—regardless of the so-called "success" of the endeavor. Success was not Paul's goal. Witness was, and witness occasionally requires blood. Consider his response to those who tried to convince him to avoid Jerusalem because of the inherent danger.

> And now, behold, I am going to Jerusalem, constrained by the Spirit, not knowing what will happen to me there, except that the Holy Spirit testifies to me in every city that

imprisonment and afflictions await me. But I do not account my life of any value nor as precious to myself, if only I may finish my course and the ministry that I received from the Lord Jesus, to testify to the gospel of the grace of God. (Acts 20:22-24)

In Acts 21 Paul responded to more of the same caution that he received in chapter 20. But this time he spoke not of "imprisonment" and "afflictions," but of "death." Luke records the exchange saying,

While we were staying for many days, a prophet named Agabus came down from Judea. And coming to us, he took Paul's belt and bound his own feet and hands and said, "Thus says the Holy Spirit, 'This is how the Jews at Jerusalem will bind the man who owns this belt and deliver him into the hands of the Gentiles.'" When we heard this, we and the people there urged him not to go up to Jerusalem. Then Paul answered, "What are you doing, weeping and breaking my heart? For I am ready not only to be imprisoned *but even to die in Jerusalem for the name of the Lord Jesus.*" (Acts 21:10-13)

The preservation of life was not Paul's highest ambition. The declaration of Christ through the demonstration of the Spirit and power was.[5] Paul understood what this required. Thus, "in [his] flesh [he was] filling up what is lacking in Christ's afflictions for the sake of His body, that is, the Church."[6] He understood this mandate from the day of his conversion when he was told of "how much he must suffer for the sake of [Jesus'] name."[7] Thus we see that Paul is the archetype of a frontier missionary. He didn't count his life as having value that exceeded that of the Gospel.

5   1 Corinthians 1-3
6   Colossians 1:24
7   Acts 9:16

Over two thousand years later, our impact in the Muslim world is contingent upon whether we will embrace this same Pauline mentality of valuing the Gospel over life. As long as we remain unwilling to bleed for the sake of Christ's fame in the Islamic world, we can be sure that there will be little impact. Thankfully, the failure of the Church to serve these precious people is being somewhat compensated for by the number of Muslims who are coming to faith each year through dreams and visions. While we should celebrate this, it mustn't be used to justify the abdication of our calling to this critical mission field. George Otis, Jr. explains the importance of a martyr-witness in Muslim nations:

> Should the Church in politically or socially trying circumstances remain covert to avoid potential eradication by forces hostile to Christianity? Or would more open confrontation with prevailing spiritual ignorance and deprivation—even if it produced Christian martyrs—be more likely to lead to evangelistic breakthroughs? Islamic fundamentalists claim that their spiritual revolution is fueled by the blood of martyrs. Is it conceivable that Christianity's failure to thrive in the Muslim world is due to the notable absence of Christian martyrs? And can the Muslim community take seriously the claims of a Church in hiding? ... The question is not whether it is wise at times to keep worship and witness discreet, but rather how long this may continue before we are guilty of "hiding our light under a bushel" ... The record shows that from Jerusalem and Damascus to Ephesus and Rome, the apostles were beaten, stoned, conspired against and imprisoned for their witness. Invitations were rare, and never the basis for their missions.[8]

We must embrace the call to the Islamic world with the conviction that martyrdom is not merely a possibility but a

8   George Otis Jr., *The Last of the Giants: Lifting the Veil on Islam and the End Times,* (Grand Rapids, MI: Chosen, 1991), 261, 263.

requirement. Those who are in bondage to Islam *need* a martyr witness to awaken them to the surpassing worth of Christ. By *not suffering* to declare the Gospel to them, our silence screams that our Gospel is not worth our dying for. A Gospel that isn't worth Christians dying for is a Gospel that isn't worth Muslims living for. Since the cost of a Muslim renouncing Allah for the sake of Christ in much of the Islamic world is rejection, opposition, persecution, estrangement, or death, they need to know that it is worth such a price. They need to know that *He* is worth it. This poses a significant challenge to the missions movement in the Western world. We must decide how we will respond to the fact that there are 1.3 billion unreached Muslims in the Islamic world who, having never been served by a crucified Church, will perish without hearing of our crucified and risen Christ.

Christian martyrdom is motivated by the believer's Spirit-wrought desire to spend eternity with his enemy that he loves enough to serve through suffering—even unto death. Until the Church displays this kind of desire to the nations, particularly, Islamic nations, her witness will fall on deaf ears, if it even falls at all.

THE LIFE AND LEGACY OF RAYMUND LULL

The premier example of such martyr-ministry to the Islamic world in the annals of Church history is that of Raymund Lull. Samuel Zwemer called him "the first missionary to the [Muslims]." He prefaced the only biography on Lull in the English language by saying,

> Stock, the editorial secretary of the Church Missionary Society, declares "there is no more heroic figure in the history of Christendom than that of Raymund Lull, the first and

perhaps the greatest missionary to Mohammedans." No complete biography of Lull exists in the English language; and since the twentieth century is to be preeminently a century of missions to Moslems, we should rescue the memory of the pioneer from oblivion. His philosophical speculations and his many books have vanished away, for he knew only in part. But his self-sacrificing love never faileth and its memory can not perish. His biography emphasizes his own motto: "He who lives by the Life cannot die." It is this part of Lull's life that has a message for us today, and calls us to win back the Mohammedan world to Christ.[9]

Lull was born in 1232 to a wealthy Catholic family on the Mediterranean island of Majorca. He grew up to become a perverse and sinful man wholly given to immorality. Then in 1265, his life changed forever, and history changed with it. While writing a "vulgar" and "erotic" song in his bedchamber, he was given an open vision of Jesus being crucified. Like Saul on the road to Damascus, Lull was arrested by a vision of glory and overcome by the wonder of the God-Man. Zwemer explains the impact of this encounter saying that

the image of the suffering Savior remained for fifty years the mainspring of his being. Love for the personal Christ filled his heart, molded his mind, inspired his pen, and made his soul long for the crown of martyrdom.[10]

Over the course of those fifty years, Lull poured himself out for the cause of Muslim evangelism. His passions were unique. No one had ever sought to stir a missions movement to Muslims before. He was the first. And he was alone. To speak of loving Muslims was unthinkable in his day, as was the idea of

9   Samuel M. Zwemer, *Raymund Lull: First Missionary to the Moslems*, Introduction.
10   *Ibid*, ch. 3.

winning them for Christ. His generation was far more concerned with subduing them with the sword.

Islamic armies had taken the Holy Land by force and were bent on gaining dominion of the whole region roundabout. "'With lightening speed,' writes J. Herbert Kane, 'they conquered Damascus (635), Antioch (636), Jerusalem (638), Caesarea (640), and Alexandria (642).' Unlike the marauding barbarians that had brought down the Roman Empire more than two centuries earlier, the Muslims often brought culture with them. It was a time when 'Arab civilization was at its height.'"[11]

In response, a succession of Popes invested the resources of Rome into bloody military conquests in attempts to stay the heavy hand of Islam. For two centuries (1095-1291) the battle raged as a series of Crusades commenced. Tens of thousands of lives were lost. And animosity between Christians and Muslims was galvanized. That animosity persists to this very day as the wounds incurred during those centuries were never healed.

In the turbulent context of social upheaval, ethnic strife, and religious war, Lull was forged as a laborer and an articulate spokesman for Islamic missions. He courageously proclaimed that the war against Islam should not be waged with the sword but through prayer, preaching, and martyrdom. Contesting the Church-sponsored military campaigns against Muslims, Lull wrote:

> I see many knights going to the Holy Land beyond the seas
> and thinking that they can acquire it by force of arms, but
> in the end all are destroyed before they attain that which

11   Ruth Tucker, *From Jerusalem to Irian Jaya: A Biographical History of Christian Missions*, (Grand Rapids, MI: Zondervan, 2010), Kindle Edition, ch. 2.

they think to have. Whence it seems to me that the con-
quest of the Holy Land ought. . . to be attempted. . . by love
and prayers, and the pouring out of tears and blood.[12]

These convictions motivated fervent prayers for the consecration of martyr-missionaries.

> I find scarcely anyone, O Lord, who out of love to Thee is
> ready to suffer martyrdom as Thou hast suffered for us. It
> appears to me agreeable to reason, if an ordinance to that
> effect could be obtained, that the monks should learn vari-
> ous languages that they might be able to go out and sur-
> render their lives in love to Thee. . . O Lord of glory, if that
> blessed day should ever be in which I might see Thy holy
> monks so influenced by zeal to glorify Thee as to go to for-
> eign lands in order to testify of Thy holy ministry, of Thy
> blessed incarnation, and of Thy bitter sufferings, that would
> be a glorious day, a day in which that glow of devotion
> would return with which the holy apostles met death for
> their Lord Jesus Christ.[13]

Motivated by love for the Islamic world and a desire for a
martyr's crown, Lull drafted plans for training centers from
which missionaries could be equipped and commissioned. He
was gripped by the vision of sending Arabic-speaking laborers
into the nations to "meet the bald monotheism of Islam face
to face with the revelation of the Father, the Son, and the Holy
Spirit." Like a number of pioneers before him, he

> viewed monasteries as the ideal training ground for evange-
> lists. He traveled widely, appealing to Church and political
> leaders to support him in the cause. King James II of Spain
> was one of those who caught his vision; and in 1276, with
> his enthusiastic support and financial contributions, Lull
> opened a monastery on Majorca with thirteen Franciscan

12 *Ibid.*
13 Samuel M Zwemer, *Raymund Lull: First Missionary to the Moslems*,
    ch. 5.

monks and a curriculum that included courses in the Arabic language and in the "geography of missions." His dream was to establish training centers all over Europe, but to do that he had to convince the Roman Catholic hierarchy of their value—no easy task. When he visited Rome on various occasions, his ideas were either ridiculed or ignored by a Church hierarchy that was more interested in worldly pleasures and personal aggrandizement than in missions. He was successful, however, in influencing a decision at the Council of Vienna to have Arabic offered in the European universities—a step that he believed would open up dialogue between Christians and Muslims.[14]

Consumed with zeal for the advance of the Gospel throughout the Islamic world, Lull made numerous trips to Tunis (a powerful center of Islamic thought) where he publicly preached the superiority of Christ over Mohammed. There he lovingly pleaded with Muslims to turn from the deceptive teachings of the Qur'an. During those years of labor he faced fierce persecution, imprisonment, and expulsion. Such opposition did not deter him but only stirred his passion with every passing year.

> A hungry man makes dispatch and takes large morsels on account of his great hunger, so Thy servant feels a great desire to die that he may glorify Thee. He hurries day and night to complete his work in order that he may give up his blood and his tears to be shed for Thee.[15]

In another place he prayed

> Men are wont to die, O Lord, from old age, the failure of natural warmth and excess of cold; but thus, if it be Thy

14 Ruth Tucker, *From Jerusalem to Irian Jaya: A Biographical History of Christian Missions*, ch. 2.
15 Samuel M. Zwemer, *Raymund Lull: First Missionary to the Moslems*, ch. 9.

will, Thy servant would not wish to die; he would prefer to die in the glow of love, even as Thou wast willing to die for him.[16]

In 1315 he, like Peter, was given the desire of his heart. Zwemer wrote

> Lull was now seventy-nine years old, and the last few years of his life must have told heavily even on so strong a frame and so brave a spirit as he possessed. His pupils and friends naturally desired that he should end his days in the peaceful pursuit of learning and the comfort of companionship. Such, however, was not Lull's wish. His ambition was to die as a missionary and not as a teacher of philosophy. Even his favorite "Ars Major" had to give way to that ars maxima expressed in Lull's own motto, "He that lives by the life cannot die."[17]

That year he returned to Bugia (a city in which he was once imprisoned for six months for preaching). "Weary of seclusion, and longing for martyrdom," Lull showed himself in the public market and began preaching. It was there that he gained the crown for which he yearned. Among a frenzied crowd he was silenced as embittered Muslims stoned him to death. Thus Zwemer wrote:

> Lull verily was a martyr in will and in deed. Not only at Bugia, when he fell asleep, but for all the years of his long life after his conversion, he was a witness to the Truth, ever ready "to fill up that which is behind of the afflictions of Christ" in his flesh "for his body's sake which is the Church."[18]

Let us receive the testimony of that martyr-missionary as

16   *Ibid.*
17   *Ibid.*
18   *Ibid.*

an invitation to walk the same narrow path. And let us pray that the Lord would raise up a generation of laborers who will lay their lives down in loving service of the Islamic world.

CHAPTER SEVEN
MARTYRDOM AND MINISTRY

In the previous chapter, we addressed the issue of martyrdom in relation to frontier missions. In this chapter, we turn our attention to martyrdom in relation to domestic ministry; that is, ministry done in a geographical area in which a Church has been established (in contrast to ministry done in a city that has never been engaged with the Gospel). Second Timothy will be our guide.

AN INTRODUCTION TO 2 TIMOTHY

With regard to practical domestic ministry, 2 Timothy is the most important book in the Bible. No other book gives more explicit attention to this service and the cost associated with it. It is an incredible gift to the Body of Christ which every minister should treasure.

One of the reasons this letter is so precious is because it is the final epistle Paul wrote before his execution. Bound with chains, incarcerated by Rome, and faced with the reality of imminent death, he wrote to a young man named Timothy. As an aged and seasoned apostle, Paul penned his final words to a comrade and fellow soldier in the fray, exhorting him to "fulfill his ministry." His words served as a plumb-line for the young pastor who was wrestling through the rigors of service to the Body of Christ and the unbelieving community round-about.

Paul, as missionary and apostle, was called to labor primarily in regions that lacked the presence of a believing community and among those who had never heard the Gospel. Listen to Paul describe the cost associated with this critical service of foundation-laying among the unreached. Because of the call, he experienced

> labors . . . imprisonments, countless beatings, and [was] often near death. Five times I received at the hands of the Jews the forty lashes less one. Three times I was beaten with rods. Once I was stoned. Three times I was shipwrecked; a night and a day I was adrift at sea; on frequent journeys, in danger from rivers, danger from robbers, danger from my own people, danger from Gentiles, danger in the city, danger in the wilderness, danger at sea, danger from false brothers; in toil and hardship, through many a sleepless night, in hunger and thirst, often without food, in cold and exposure. And, apart from other things, there is the daily pressure on me of my anxiety for all the churches. (2 Corinthians 11:23-28)

Timothy's assignment was different. He was appointed to labor in relationship to an established Church (which Paul most likely planted years before). While he, like Paul, was also called to preach to unbelievers, Timothy's work was not among those who had *never* heard, but among those who had heard but had *rejected* the Gospel message. Paul's exhortations to Timothy were given in light of the pressures, dangers, and difficulties associated with that critical ministry. While we are *all* called to value frontier missions among the unreached and unengaged, most believers are called to actually minister among unbelievers in context to an established Church. A *minority* will travel to distant nations to witness to those who have never heard in a tongue that is not their own. The *majority* will remain at home and witness to their own people in their own language. It is essential that we value both of these mandates and recognize that God dispenses various gifts to those with various assignments. And as we acknowledge the importance of both, we must understand the role of hardship, suffering, persecution, and martyrdom in context of both. So before we look at 2 Timothy, I offer what I believe is the apostolic perspective on persecution and martyrdom relating to domestic ministry.

THE DANGERS OF DOMESTIC MINISTRY

Some may be inclined to believe that frontier missions is somehow more dangerous than domestic ministry. Depending on what country we are from, it can be. But Church history suggests that, if it is, it is more of a statement of the weakness of the Church's witness than the nature of the dangers associated with local evangelism. Historically speaking, the majority of martyrs have been slain by their own people in their own lands *because* of their response to the break-through ministry of frontier missionaries. For example, more Indonesian believers were killed in the 1990s than were foreign missionaries.

Once the Gospel had penetrated because of a frontier missionary, the level of danger was heightened, not minimized. Why? Because indigenous believers were now bearing witness among their own people. At the start, missionary families were being stabbed in their sleep. Afterwards, entire Churches were being burnt to the ground and their indigenous members hacked to death. As recently as December 2011, prominent news agencies worldwide were reporting the vicious attacks against Christians in Nigeria and Iraq. In both cases, it was the result of domestic ministry as the murderers lashed out against the indigenous Church.

With this in view, it becomes apparent that bearing witness to the Gospel in spatial proximity to an established Church doesn't mean that it will be safe. Sometimes it is just the opposite. Western nations like the United States, Canada, and England (where the Church is weakening in her witness and diminishing in her number of fervent members) are exceptions to the norm. Faithful domestic ministry in nations like Syria, Indonesia, Columbia, and Bangladesh is just as dangerous as frontier missions in these same nations by virtue of the fact that the cost of publicly acknowledging allegiance to Jesus of Nazareth is scorned. It is one thing for a foreign missionary to be rejected by a community that is not his own; it is another thing for an indigenous believer to be rejected by his own community. Who is to say which is more costly? I, for one, am not prepared to say.

The fiercest persecution recorded in the book of Acts was experienced by the established Church in Jerusalem. The same also applies to the executions of the first martyrs. Stephen and James were killed in their hometown by those who spoke their own language. Interestingly, this persecution was the seedbed for frontier missions. Acts 8 makes this clear. After describing Stephen's death, Luke records that

> Saul approved of his execution. And there arose on that day a great persecution against the church in Jerusalem, and

> they were all scattered throughout the regions of Judea and Samaria, except the apostles. Devout men buried Stephen and made great lamentation over him. But Saul was ravaging the church, and entering house after house, he dragged off men and women and committed them to prison. Now those who were scattered went about preaching the word. Philip went down to the city of Samaria and proclaimed to them the Christ. (Acts 8:1-5)

"On *that* day" that Stephen was killed in his hometown while engaging in domestic ministry among his own people (he was serving the poor through food distribution),[1] "great persecution" broke out "against the Church in Jerusalem." The community was "ravaged" "house after house," and "men and women" were imprisoned. The persecution of one man was the wick that set off the explosion of persecution against believers in an entire city. *This* was the result of the domestic ministry of Stephen and the believers in Jerusalem.

Yet look at the fruit. "On *that* day" that the persecution broke out, "those who were scattered went about preaching the word." "Philip went down to the city of Samaria" preaching Christ and Him crucified. This passage marks a significant moment in the history of the early Church. This was the beginning of frontier missions, just as Jesus commanded in Acts 1:8: "in Jerusalem, Judea, Samaria, and to the ends of the earth." Acts 11 expounds on the fruit of the persecution that broke out in Jerusalem after Stephen's death.

> Now those who were scattered because of the persecution that arose over Stephen traveled as far as Phoenicia and Cyprus and Antioch, speaking the word to no one except Jews. But there were some of them, men of Cyprus and Cyrene, who on coming to Antioch spoke to the Hellenists also, preaching the Lord Jesus. And the hand of the Lord

1   See Acts 6-7

> was with them, and a great number who believed turned to the Lord. The report of this came to the ears of the church in Jerusalem, and they sent Barnabas to Antioch. When he came and saw the grace of God, he was glad, and he exhorted them all to remain faithful to the Lord with steadfast purpose, for he was a good man, full of the Holy Spirit and of faith. And a great many people were added to the Lord. (Acts 11:19-24)

Note the shift in strategy between 11:19 and 11:20. Those who were being scattered to new frontiers beyond Jerusalem were still only speaking to Jews. The Gospel had not yet penetrated the veil of another culture. "But," Luke records, "there were some of them . . . who on coming to Antioch spoke to the Hellenists also, preaching the Lord Jesus." This was the birth of frontier missions. The cause? Persecution against an established Church because of domestic ministry. The catalyst? The martyrdom of *one man*—a domestic minister laboring among his own people.

If we model our ministry efforts after the precedents set by the early Church in the book of Acts, then we must conclude:

> That domestic ministry is no less dangerous than frontier ministry.

> That persecution against domestic ministry (including martyrdom) is the greatest catalyst for frontier missions.

> That whether we are called to domestic ministry or frontier missions, persecution and martyrdom should be expected.

Moreover, we should view persecution and martyrdom as more than just the natural backlash of faithful and courageous domestic ministry and frontier missions. We should also acknowledge it as a divine strategy that God employs to mature the Church and advance her witness among unreached and unengaged peoples, cultures, and regions. If we view the stoning of Stephen as nothing more than satanic rage against the Church and fail to see the providential hand of God in his death, as well as in the persecution that followed, then we don't see it rightly. With this theological and missiological paradigm established, the message of 2 Timothy will make much more sense than without it.

THE CENTRAL MESSAGE OF 2 TIMOTHY

The central message of 2 Timothy is found in 1:6-8. These three verses frame the message of this weighty epistle.

> For this reason I remind you to fan into flame the gift of God, which is in you through the laying on of my hands, for God gave us a spirit not of fear but of power and love and self-control. Therefore do not be ashamed of the testimony about our Lord, nor of me his prisoner, but share in suffering for the gospel by the power of God. (2 Timothy 1:6-8)

The phrase "share in suffering for the Gospel by the power of God" is the primary thrust of Paul's appeal to this young domestic laborer. There are three reasons why I believe this is clear.

First, we are able to see that a thread of redemptive suffering for the sake of the Gospel runs throughout the whole book. Paul mentions the issue of suffering no less than fourteen times. This is a rather incredible number considering the book is only four chapters long. *Thematically speaking, 2 Timothy is about suffering.* The following fourteen passages make this clear.

> "Onesiphorus . . . was not ashamed of my chains" (1:16).
>
> "Share in suffering as a good soldier of Christ Jesus" (2:3).

"I am suffering [for the Gospel], bound with chains as a criminal" (2:9).

"I endure everything for the sake of the elect" (2:10).

"If we endure, we will also reign with him" (2:12).

"Do your best to present yourself . . . a worker who has no need to be ashamed" (2:15).

"And the Lord's servant must . . . patiently endure evil" (2:24).

"In the last days there will come times of difficulty" (3:1).

"You . . . have followed my . . . persecutions and sufferings" (3:10).

"All who desire to live a godly life in Christ Jesus will be persecuted" (3:12).

"As for you . . . endure suffering" (4:5).

"I am already being poured out as a drink offering, and the time of my departure has come" (4:6).

"I have fought the good fight" (4:7).

"At my first defense no one came to stand by me, but all deserted me" (4:16).

Second, as Paul lay in a filthy jail cell awaiting execution, he was embodying and demonstrating the exhortation to "fan into flames" the fire of consecration and courage. When Paul told Timothy to "share in suffering for the Gospel" in verse 8, he was asking him to embrace the same kind of opposition that he himself was experiencing for bearing faithful witness to the Gospel. It is profound that this verse about suffering comes on the heels of the exhortation to "fan into flames" the fire of fervency. The conjunction word "therefore" between the sentences is designed to point us to the end for which the flames were first kindled and intended to be fanned: (1) That Timothy would overcome ungodly shame as he testified of the Lord Jesus and

(2) that Timothy would lay down his life to suffer with Paul. Put those two together and you have this message: "Timothy! Take up the courage that is available to you through the indwelling Holy Spirit and come with me to suffer gloriously!" *Exegetically speaking, 2 Timothy is about suffering.*

Third, all of Paul's advice, admonition and exhortation are aimed at preparing Timothy to stand firm in the face of pressure. This is the end for which Paul is laboring to edify him. If Timothy stood faithful in the face of opposition, so would those he was called to serve. In Paul's mind, this was a corporate issue. Paul was encouraging this young man to look upon the pressures and afflictions that had fallen upon him as an example of what he should expect and anticipate due to his high calling. This letter to Timothy wasn't about Paul's explaining doctrine, as in Romans or Ephesians, but about calling Timothy to a sacrificial lifestyle, which was being modeled through Paul's own distresses as he wrote from prison. If this was faithfully modeled through Timothy, the Church would thrive. *Pastorally speaking, 2 Timothy is about suffering.*

EMBRACING THE BIBLICAL THEOLOGY OF SUFFERING FOR THE GOSPEL

In this precious book, we have been given a paradigm for the necessity of suffering for the Gospel's sake. This theological framework is essential to understand Paul's letter to Timothy. The word "suffer" is used six times. But the reality of "suffering" occurs around fourteen times. These fourteen verses give perspective to the call to "share in suffering for the Gospel by the power of God."

Timothy could only *partake of* the sort of suffering to

which he was called "by the power of God" (1:8). This is an important point. All too often the power of God is exalted as the means by which we are to *escape* suffering. But this idea is counterintuitive to the apostolic mind. Paul understood that God grants power for the healing of the diseases *and* the enduring of death. So while he demonstrated the power of God by casting out demons and raising the dead, he *also* demonstrated the power of God by enduring suffering and ultimately embracing martyrdom. We, too, must affirm both.

When we see 1:6-8 as the principle burden of the book, a number of contextually important truths shine forth. First, Paul was writing to a timid young man bogged down by his own weaknesses and insecurities who had a profound calling on his life. That makes this book especially important and relevant for young people. And second, Paul was writing to prepare Timothy to live courageously in the face of the pressures that were bearing upon him, as well as the pressures yet to come. Young people who desire to run their race with endurance and give a faithful witness should hide Paul's words in their hearts.

> Where are the young men and women of this generation who will hold their lives cheap and be faithful even unto death? Where are those who will lose their lives for Christ's sake—flinging them away for love of him? Where are those who will live dangerously and be reckless in his service? Where are his lovers—those who love him and the souls of men more than their own reputations or comfort or very life?

> Where are the men who say 'no' to self, who take up Christ's cross to bear it after him, who are willing to be nailed to it in college or office, home or mission field, who are willing, if need be, to bleed, to suffer and to die on it?

> Where are the adventurers, the explorers, the buccaneers

for God, who count one human soul of far greater value than the rise or fall of an empire? Where are the men who are willing to pay the price of vision?[2]

Perhaps you are bogged down by insecurities, trying awkwardly to steward the call of God on your life (as I am). Because of our immaturity and lack of tenacity, we, like Timothy, may feel it's easier to back off from that which we have been called. This makes 2 Timothy invaluable to me personally. As a young man who is wrestling through the rigors of faithful Gospel ministry, I receive it as a plumb line. Further, I believe that this generation of young laborers must embrace the New Testament theology of suffering if we truly desire to be faithful in our ministry. Unfortunately, this is one of the most underdeveloped subjects in contemporary preaching and teaching, and much of the Church (particularly in the West) is languishing because of it. Together, we must recover the glory of this valuable message.

To conclude this chapter on the role of suffering, persecution, and martyrdom within faithful domestic Gospel ministry, I leave you with an excerpt from John G. Lake's sermon, *A Trumpet Call,* which was preached at a commissioning service of South African missionaries in the early 1900s. Lake was addressing a generation of young martyr-missionaries, calling them to that which Paul called Timothy. The sermon can be read in its entirety in Appendix I.

Beloved, we have lost the character of consecration . . . God is trying to restore it in our day.

Do you know why God poured out His Spirit in South Africa like He did no where else in the world? There was a reason. This example will illustrate. We had one hundred and

2   Howard Guinness, *Sacrifice*, (Chicago: IVP, 1947), 59-60.

twenty-five men out on the field at one time. We were a very young institution and were not known in the world. South Africa is seven thousand miles from any European country. It is ten thousand miles by way of England to the United States. Our finances got so low, under the awful assault we were compelled to endure, that there came a time I could not even mail to these workers, at the end of the month, a $10 bill. It got so I could not send them $2. The situation was desperate. What was I to do? Under these circumstances I did not want to take the responsibility of leaving men and their families on the frontier without real knowledge of what the conditions were.

Some of us at headquarters sold our clothes in some cases, sold certain pieces of furniture out of the house, sold anything we could sell, to bring those hundred and twenty-five workers off the field for a conference.

One night in the progress of the conference I was invited by a committee to leave the room for a minute or two. The conference wanted to have a word by themselves. So I stepped out to a restaurant for a cup of coffee, and came back. Then I came back in, I found they had rearranged the chairs in an oval, with a little table at one end, and on the table was the bread and wine. Old Father Vanderwall, speaking for the company said, "Brother John, during your absence we have come to a conclusion. We have made our decision. We want you to serve the LORD's Supper. We are going back to our fields. We are going back if our wives die. We are going back if we have to starve. We are going back if we have to walk back. We are going back if our children die. We are going back if we die ourselves. We have but one request. If we die, we want you to come and bury us."

The next year I buried twelve of those men, along with sixteen of their wives and children.

In my judgment, not one of them, if they had a few things a white man needs to eat, could but what might have lived. Friends, when you want to find out why the power of

God came down from heaven in South Africa like it never came down before, since the time of the apostles, there is your answer.[3]

3   Roberts Liardon, *John G. Lake: The Complete Collection of His Life Teachings,* (New Kensington, PA: Whitaker House, 1999), 36-41.

Chapter Eight
Martyrdom and the End

In this chapter (and much of the next), we are going to focus on the call to martyrdom at the end of the age.

The Church in the generation of the Lord's return will be confronted with the issue of martyrdom in a dramatic way in the midst of a global "trouble such as never has been."[1] The scope and magnitude of this final hour of persecution will eclipse all those that have preceded it. The impact of this unparalleled violence will be such that believers from "every nation, from all tribes and peoples and languages" will suffer and lose their lives during the final "great tribulation."[2] Never in history has there been a period in which believers were slain in every nation within the same concentrated time frame.

The New Testament emphasis on martyrdom in the years leading up to Christ's return is rather incredible. In most chapters where the main trends and events concerning the end of

1   Daniel 12:1-7; Jeremiah 30:5-7; Matthew 24:9-31
2   Revelation 7:9-14

the age are introduced, the issue of martyrdom is mentioned. Understanding the centrality of this issue in relation to God's eschatological purposes will be indispensable to the Church as she prepares to "stand" in the face of the coming storm.

Introduction to Matthew 24-25

While there are numerous passages that demonstrate the prominence of martyrdom in the end-times we are going to limit ourselves to Matthew 24:9-14. These verses contain a number of statements relevant to our study. But first, a few preliminary observations about Matthew 24-25 are in order.

While Matthew 24 and 25 are divided into two chapters in our Bible, it is one sermon that should be read and understood as a unified whole. It is often referred to as "The Olivet Discourse" as it was delivered on the Mount of Olives overlooking the city of Jerusalem. The central message of Matthew 24-25 is "the signs of the end of the age and [Jesus'] return" (24:3). It was spoken to young adults[3] who desired to understand the consummation of natural history.

In verses 1-2, Jesus declared that the Temple would be destroyed. According to the Old Testament, the destruction of the Temple was *the* great event[4] that was to signal the "time of the end" (Daniel 11:31; cf. 12:1-13) and the final "trouble such as never has been" (Daniel 12:1-7; Jeremiah 30:5-7; Matthew 24:15-31). This trouble will immediately precede the "salvation" (Jeremiah 30:5-7) and "deliverance" of Israel and the

3   Traditionally, the disciples have been represented in art and film as grown men. This is very unlikely. When Jesus called them to follow Him, it was in accordance with the rabbinical custom of calling and training young men for the ministry. The twelve disciples were probably in their late teens and early twenties.

4   See Isaiah 63:18; Daniel 8:13-14; 9:26-27; 11:30-12:13; Matthew 24:15-31; 2 Thessalonians 2:1-11; Revelation 11:1-2

resurrection of the righteous "dead" (Daniel 12:1-3). As the disciples were aware of these prophecies, and understood that the destruction of the Temple and the "time of the end" were inextricably bound together (Daniel 12:1-13), they responded in verse 3 by asking "when" these events would come to pass and "what the signs" of their nearness would be. From 24:4 through to the end of chapter 25, Jesus answers their question.

Jesus' response to their question can be divided into two sections: Prophetic Teaching (24:1-31) and Pastoral Teaching (24:32-25:46). Prophetically, Jesus declares trends and events. Then pastorally, He explains how we should live in light of those trends and events. For Jesus, the issue of the end of the age was clearly a pastoral issue. Sadly much of the Western Church does not agree with Him.

In the first (prophetic) section we find no use of metaphors, parables, or enigmatic teachings that we find elsewhere in the Gospels. In Matthew 24:1-31 *Jesus speaks in plain language about literal events* that would have their violent inception in "Judea" and touch "all nations" before "the end." These thirty-one verses require no interpretation. They mean what they say. The second section is much different.

In the second (pastoral) section (Matthew 24:32-25:46) Jesus speaks in parables and metaphors saying, "the Kingdom of heaven *is like...*" He alludes to fig trees, the days of Noah, servants, virgins, sheep, goats, and more. These parabolic teachings were intended to complement the straightforward prophetic information given in 24:1-31.

When the plain meaning of the prophecy in the first half of Jesus' sermon isn't properly understood, the power and purpose of the parables will be lost. We mustn't read these chapters as separate teachings on two different occasions and must be careful not to stress points within it that aren't honoring to or harmonious with the sermon as a whole. Unfortunately, this happens all too often with this precious passage as ministers isolate a parable and apply it in a general way. Therefore, preachers and teachers should refrain from speaking on the parables and emphasizing their messages if they don't understand and recognize the context in which they are to be read. Few passages have suffered as much abuse at the hands of ministers as Matthew 24-25. This is primarily because the text is so often inappropriately emphasized due to ignorance of the overall message. The parables and pastoral exhortations were all given in context to the "then" (25:1) and the "those days" (24:29) of the "birth pains" (24:8) and "great tribulation" (24:21) at "the end of the age" (24:3). This eschatological framework must be faithfully emphasized.

Below is a three-part outline of Matthew 24-25. This broad perspective is essential to a correct understanding of verses 9-14 and the issue of martyrdom.

1. **Jesus' Statement about the Temple and the Disciple's Question (24:1-3)**
   a. Jesus Prophesies the Destruction of the Temple (24:1-2)
   b. The Disciples Ask About the Signs of the End (24:3)

2. **Jesus' Answer: Prophetic Teaching**
   Trends and Events that Will Precede Jesus' Return (24:4-31)
   a. Global Social and Ecological Disturbances Called Birth Pains (24:4-8)
   b. Social Pressures that Correspond to the Birth Pains (24:9-14)

c. The <u>Commencement</u> of the Great Tribulation (24:15-20)

d. The <u>Unequaled Severity</u> of the Great Tribulation (24:21-28)

e. The <u>Conclusion</u> of the Great Tribulation (24:29-31)

3. Jesus' Answer: Pastoral Teaching

Seven Parables about Preparation (24:32-25:46)

a. The Fig Tree (24:33-35)

b. The Days of Noah (24:36-41)

c. The Thief (24:42-44)

d. The Faithful and Wise Servant (24:45-51)

e. The Ten Virgins and the Coming Bridegroom (25:1-13)

f. The Talents (25:14-30)

g. The Least of Jesus' Brethren (25:31-46)

The Centrality of Martyrdom in the Olivet Discourse

Now with the context clearly in view, let us focus on 24:9-14 where Jesus stresses the centrality and prominence of martyrdom in the generation of His return. After describing earthquakes, military conflict, famine, and social disturbance as the preliminary signs that would signal the early stages of the end-time crisis ("...these are but the *beginning* of the birth pains" [24:8]) Jesus said that

> *Then* they will deliver you up to tribulation and put you to death, and you will be hated by all nations for my name's sake. And then many will fall away and betray one another and hate one another. And many false prophets will arise and lead many astray. And because lawlessness will be increased, the love of many will grow cold. But the one who

endures to the end will be saved. And this gospel of the kingdom will be proclaimed throughout the whole world as a testimony to all nations, and then the end will come. (Matthew 24:9-14)

The word "then" in verse 9 is important (see also 24:29 and 25:1). It gives us insight into the timing and nature of the outbreak of the final persecution of the saints. "Then" refers to the pressures that will be mounting in the nations as the frequency and intensity of "the birth pains" grip the Earth like a woman entering hard labor ("...the tribulation of *those days.*" [24:29]). "Then" refers to the climactic season of history that leads up to and culminates in the violent inception of "the great tribulation" (24:21-22) in "Judea" (24:15-16) and ultimately the bodily return of Jesus to the Earth.

"*Then*," in that turbulent hour of mounting crisis, "tribulation," "death," "hatred," "falling away," "betrayal," and "deception" will be the primary "signs" of the times. But make note of these two critical truths, dear saint: (1) this great violence is centered around Jesus' name ("...for my name's sake.") and (2) this great violence will impact every nation ("...you will be hated by all nations."). It is imperative that we observe and affirm both of these realities. The nature of the final conflict of the age-ending persecution is Christ-centered. And the scope of it will be unprecedented. On that note, it is important to address a potential stumbling block with regard to the nature of the Olivet Discourse.

There are many who argue that Matthew 24-25 was fulfilled in and around AD 70 with the Roman invasion of Jerusalem and the destruction of the Temple. Many godly men and women believe this. They teach that the Olivet Discourse is not about the future concerning the end of this present age, but rather the past concerning the end of the *Jewish* age. Every believer who wishes to honor the Word of God should heartily reject this teaching. It is a false doctrine that will have serious consequences in the generation of the Lord's return.

The fall of Jerusalem in AD 70 was not persecution against the Church. It was a military campaign against Israel. In fact, much of the Christian population of Judea fled to the surrounding wilderness regions when the invasions began and escaped the violence. Jesus taught that one of the most conspicuous trends and events that would distinguish the final unequaled tribulation (24:21-22) from the historical continuum of tribulation (Acts 14:22; Revelation 1:9) will be the concentrated persecution of believers for "[His] name's sake." The persecution spoken of in Matthew 24-25 that will impact "all nations." The intellectual dishonesty required to apply such a prophecy finally and ultimately to AD 70 is astounding. Considering that the Great Commission had just begun three decades prior to the fall of Jerusalem, we should find it strange when a preacher claims that the trends and events described in the Olivet Discourse had their fulfillment in the first century.[5] They most certainly did not.

THREE MONUMENTAL EVENTS IN THE GENERATION OF THE LORD'S RETURN CONCERNING MISSIONS AND MARTYRDOM

These six verses (24:9-14) contain three monumental events

5   Some cite Colossians 1:23 and Romans 1:8 as evidence that the Gospel had already been proclaimed to all nations in the first century. This author believes this to be a poor handling of the text and recommends John Piper's article, "Has the Gospel Been Preached to the Whole Creation Already?" from *Desiring God* (website), http://www.desiringgod. org/blog/posts/has-the-gospel-been-preached-to-the-whole-creation-already.

that the Church among the nations must understand. While all three have already been introduced in a limited way, I want to acknowledge them individually as propositional truths and further expound upon their significance. We are going to work our way backwards from verse 14 to verse 9.

1. The Penetration of the Gospel in Every Nation (24:14)

Matthew 24:14 is an incredible prophecy that should bolster us with great courage and boldness. Jesus says that, "this Gospel of the Kingdom *will* be proclaimed throughout *the whole world* as a testimony to *all nations . . .*" It will! It must! There will come a day when every tribe, tongue, nation, and people group will have heard the name of Jesus and the wonder of the Gospel. Beloved, consider Matthew 24:14. The "whole world" will hear the Gospel. And "all nations" will receive a witness.

What's more, Jesus declared that the penetration of the Gospel in every nation is one of the few conditions for "the end." He has bound the issue of His return to the fate of the unreached. The two are inseparable—the one being contingent upon the other. According to Christ's own word, He *will not return* until every tribe and tongue have heard "this Gospel of the Kingdom."

As was stated in chapter five, while the number of unreached people groups at this present hour is not small (over six thousand), leaders of many of the largest missions organizations are stating confidently that the task can and most likely will be fulfilled within the lifetime of our children. Think about the significance of that. Your children could live to see the remaining unreached people groups engaged with the Gospel. We could be the generation that completes what the disciples began in Jerusalem two thousand years ago (Acts 1:8). If not us, then almost certainly our children. But either way, according to Matthew 24:14, we are on the threshold of the final "tribulation" (24:4-31) that will cover the Earth once the Gospel has penetrated these currently unreached and unengaged nations. Saint, this is no peripheral matter!

2. The Provocation of Global Hatred in Every Nation (24:9)

While the thought of engaging every tribe and tongue with the Gospel of the Kingdom in our lifetime should invigorate and excite us, it is important to observe the context in which the prophecy of 24:14 was given. The penetration of the Gospel into all nations will result in the provocation of all nations. While many from every tribe and tongue will turn and put their faith in Christ before His return, we must understand that this great ingathering of souls will come about in the midst of all the nations of the Earth raging.

> Then they will deliver you up to tribulation and put you to death, and you will be hated by all nations for My name's sake. And then many will fall away and betray one another and hate one another. And many false prophets will arise and lead many astray. And because lawlessness will be increased, the love of many will grow cold. But the one who endures to the end will be saved.

Ponder these statements individually: "*They* will deliver you up." "*They* will put you to death." "You will be hated by *all nations.*" Note the words "they" and "all nations." The final persecution of the Church will be a worldwide reality. "All nations" will "deliver up" believers and "put them to death."

These are not ambiguous ideas. They are emphatic

proclamations of global rage, worldwide violence, and unprecedented persecution. While some may find this difficult to believe considering the measure of safety enjoyed by Christians in much of the Earth at this time, the Word of God compels us to lean upon the sure word of prophecy and not our own reasoning based on present circumstances. The scope and magnitude of the Church's end-time suffering as described in passages like these is staggering. The thought vexes the modern mind. We find it difficult to believe that such brutality and injustice could truly cover the Earth to this degree because of how progressive, sophisticated, and tolerant many nations are in which we live. But remember, dear reader, that the seedbed of one of the most gruesome atrocities in human history was Germany in the 1930s and 1940s. Arguably the most cultured and socially impressive nations on Earth dreamed up the systematic annihilation of European Jewry. The fact that the gross injustice of the Holocaust had its inception in the cultured society of twentieth-century Germany stands as an apologetic against those who would hastily dismiss the idea of global persecution in the future.

3. The Persecution of Believers in Every Nation (24:9)

The Gospel will penetrate every nation before Jesus returns. It is likely that it will occur within your lifetime or that of your children. And when it does, the greatest persecution that the Church has ever known will break out against believers in every nation. Jesus was clear: We will be hated by all nations. As a result, we will be persecuted in all nations. We must understand this, proclaim it, and prepare for it. The consequences of *not preparing* for this will be severe for us, and those we love.

The impact of the violence described in Matthew 24:9-14 will be "falling away" and "love growing cold." As the Gospel penetrates unreached peoples and nations, many, by grace, through faith, will join themselves to Jesus. Yet in the midst of the overwhelming scourge, we are also told that many will wander away into apostasy due to the intense persecution at hand.

Due to the fact that persecution against Christians will break out in "all nations" with the advance of the Gospel "throughout the whole world," those who turn to Christ in that hour will do so at the risk of martyrdom. Thus, as it was at the start so it will be at the end: that the call to Jesus will literally be a call to die. We would be hard pressed to exaggerate the seriousness of these realities and their relevance to the Church in the generation of the Lord's return.

INNUMERABLE MARTYRS WILL COME OUT OF THE GREAT TRIBULATION

While on the island of Patmos, John was shown the magnitude of this coming season of persecution during the final tribulation. The vision was breathtaking.

> After this I looked, and behold, a great multitude that no one could number, from every nation, from all tribes and peoples and languages, standing before the throne and before the Lamb, clothed in white robes, with palm branches in their hands, and crying out with a loud voice, "Salvation belongs to our God who sits on the throne, and to the Lamb!" And all the angels were standing around the throne and around the elders and the four living creatures, and they fell on their faces before the throne and worshiped God, saying, "Amen! Blessing and glory and wisdom and thanksgiving and honor and power and might be to our God forever and ever! Amen."

> Then one of the elders addressed me, saying, "Who are these, clothed in white robes, and from where have they come?" I said to him, "Sir, you know." And he said to me, "These are the ones coming out of the great tribulation. They have washed their robes and made them white in the blood of the Lamb." (Revelation 7:9-14)

The scene is incredible. Men, women, and children from every nation, tribe, people, and language together in one accord declaring their great love for the One who redeemed them with His royal blood. Like a sea of faces stretching as far as the apostle's eye could see, the congregation was innumerable. John had never seen so many people in one place and surely never from such diverse ethnic backgrounds. As he stood in awe of the sublime sight before him, one of the twenty-four elders approached him and asked whether he knew where these robed saints had come from. The elder knew the answer, but he wanted to make sure John knew. And he wanted to make sure that we know. So he answered his own question, saying, "These are the ones coming out of the great tribulation." The "great tribulation" is not the same as the historic "tribulation" spoken of in Revelation 1:7 or in 2:9, that historical continuum of suffering that the Church has faced since the beginning. The tribulation from which that innumerable multitude will emerge is the same "great tribulation" that Jesus spoke about in Matthew 24:9-31; it is that tribulation which begins with global "birth pains" and the "desolation" of Jerusalem, and culminates in the shaking of the cosmos and the bodily return of Jesus to the Earth. Take careful note of how Jesus described it.

> For then there will be great tribulation, such as has not been from the beginning of the world until now, no, and never will be. And if those days had not been cut short, no human being would be saved. But for the sake of the elect those

days will be cut short. (Matthew 24:21-22)

That hour of tribulation will be entirely unprecedented in scope and magnitude. It will require Jesus' physical intervention to bring it to a close. Yet out of it the Church of Jesus Christ will give the greatest martyr-witness she has ever had the privilege to give. The Church will not be a passive spectator of that hour, having escaped beforehand in a secret rapture. No. The Church will come *out of* that tribulation having given a faithful martyr-witness in the midst of it.

CONCLUSION

Martyrdom will be a premier sign of the times in the generation of the Lord's return. As the Church, we must faithfully declare it and prepare accordingly. In the next chapter, we will delve further into the subject of martyrdom in an eschatological context in order to show how God intends to bring His people into maturity through the crucible of persecution and suffering.

Chapter Nine
Martyrdom and Maturity

Up to this point we have considered the call to martyrdom almost entirely in individualistic terms expounding on Paul's declaration in Philippians 1:21 where he wrote, "for *me* to live is Christ and to die is gain." We have focused on the implications of the message as it pertains to "*me*;" that is, the *individual* believer. However, in this closing chapter, we will grapple with the *corporate* and *collective* terms with which martyrdom is emphasized in the New Testament, and thereby consider how this message applies to *us, communally*, as the Church body. There are few places where these corporate terms are used more overtly than Revelation 12:11. Here we read of

> *they* [who] have conquered [Satan] by the blood of the Lamb and by the word of *their* testimony, for *they* loved not *their* lives even unto death.

In order to rightly understand the significance of this prophetic declaration about the Church's corporate victory over the Evil One, we need to read it in its context. The saints in

117

Revelation 12:11 who are given the opportunity to love not their lives unto death are those who will suffer under the heavy hand of a tyrannical ruler John refers to as "the beast."[1] In one of his epistles John calls him "the antichrist."[2] Paul refers to him as "the man of sin;" and "the son of perdition."[3] In Daniel's vision, he was called "a cruel" and "vile man."[4] Although he has yet to be revealed, this man spoken of *is a real person* (as we are told Christ will personally execute him at His appearing), and he will unleash a violent persecution against the saints of God. The martyrs of Revelation 12:11 are those on whom the beast will "wage war" during the "great tribulation" described in Revelation 13:5-7.

> And the beast was given a mouth uttering haughty and blasphemous words, and it was allowed to exercise authority for forty-two months. It opened its mouth to utter blasphemies against God, blaspheming his name and his dwelling, that is, those who dwell in heaven. Also it was allowed to make war on the saints *and to conquer them.* And authority was given it over every tribe and people and language and nation. (Revelation 13:5-7)

Note the word "*conquer*" in both 13:7 and 12:11. In Revelation 13:7, Satan *conquers the saints* by killing them. In Revelation 12:11, the saints *conquer Satan* by being killed by him. We overcome by being overcome by him. Herein lies the true path to maturity—through the corporate embrace of martyrdom. It is *through death* that the wisdom of God is displayed and the powers and principalities of the air confounded and ultimately defeated. While these realities are rarely emphasized

1   Revelation 13
2   1 John 2
3   2 Thessalonians 2
4   Daniel 7, 8, and 11

in contemporary preaching and teaching, they are profoundly biblical, and should therefore be declared as such.

The Call to Martyrdom and the Corporate Church

Jesus' call for us to "lose our lives" is central not only to our personal discipleship and embrace of the Great Commission, but is indispensable to the function and calling of the corporate Church. In the New Testament, the issue of Christ-likeness and maturity in the life of the individual was almost always framed by the vision of "mature manhood" as a unified "body."[5] Until we understand, embrace, and walk out this holy message as a united people, we are living beneath the intentions of God.

In Revelation 2, in one of the letters to the seven Churches, Jesus addressed the entire congregation at Smyrna concerning the issue of martyrdom.

> "And to the angel of the church in Smyrna write: 'The words of the first and the last, who died and came to life. I know your tribulation and your poverty (but you are rich) and the slander of those who say that they are Jews and are not, but are a synagogue of Satan. Do not fear what you are about to suffer. Behold, the devil is about to throw some of you into prison, that you may be tested, and for ten days you will have tribulation. Be faithful unto death, and I will give you the crown of life. He who has an ear, let him hear what the Spirit says to the churches. The one who conquers will not be hurt by the second death.'" (Revelation 2:8-11)

After declaring Himself to be One who "died and came to life," He charged them prophetically as a Church body to embrace death as a means of living before Him in faithfulness and devotion. First, Christ acknowledged their present sufferings

5   Ephesians 4:11-13

("tribulation," "poverty," and "slander") so as to remind them that the injustices that they were facing had not escaped His loving and attentive gaze. He was aware of what was happening, and He was with them in the midst of it—not as an idle bystander, but as One who had drunk deeply of the same bitter cup. Following this, He charged them "not to fear" this "suffering" before warning them of a *yet future* season of persecution which would include imprisonment and even execution. Finally, He gave the central exhortation of the letter: *"Be faithful unto death, and I will give you the crown of life."* Why? Because "the one who conquers will not be hurt by the second death." They will live forevermore!

Every line in this letter to the Church in Smyrna is incredible and deserves sober contemplation. But I want to emphasize one issue in particular that we would be wise to consider. Namely, that Jesus called an entire Church in a particular city to embrace a vision for faithfulness unto death. For many of us, especially those of us in the West, we find it hard to imagine Jesus exhorting an entire congregation to embrace martyrdom. But as we can plainly see, He did. Knowing our Lord to be the same "yesterday, today, and forever," we can be sure that His esteem for this holy way has not changed, and this message is as relevant to us as a corporate people as it was then. Further, though we recognize that Jesus did not exhort *all* of the seven Churches concerning martyrdom, this in no way diminishes the seriousness of His exhortation to Smyrna. If He called *a* Church to embrace a vision for faithfulness unto death, it would be foolish to assume that He doesn't in a very real way call *the* Church to embrace this same vision.

Our personal and individual confession that "to live is Christ and to die is gain" is intended by God to be expressed collectively, particularly at the end of the age when God intends to bring the Church into an appointed "fullness" in the midst of the greatest opposition she has ever known. In light of the pressures associated with the end of the age, and in light of the New Testament's emphasis on the eschatological maturity of the Church, it is imperative that we integrate the theology of martyrdom into the fabric of our ecclesiology. God intends the Bride of Christ to be a martyr-Church. Therefore, we maintain that this message concerning "faithfulness unto death" is foundational to Christian living and essential for the Church's health and development on a corporate level. Without this vision for the maturity of the collective Body of Christ, through faithfulness unto death, we will invariably miss much of what God intends to accomplish in His people through the crucible of suffering, persecution, and tribulation; all of which will become increasingly prominent in every nation before the Lord's return.[6]

The Journey into Maturity and the Fellowship of Suffering

The New Testament is rife with statements concerning the corporate maturity of the Church. Jesus preached about it[7] and prayed for it.[8] Paul taught about it.[9] The writer of Hebrews made much of it.[10] And Peter longed for it.[11] In the minds of the apostles, the issue was integral to the apostolic faith. We are the "*Body* of Christ," and as such, we are

6   Matthew 24:9-14; Revelation 6:9-11; 7:9-14; 12:7-12
7   Matthew 16:18-19
8   John 17:20-26
9   Ephesians 4:11-15
10   Hebrews 6:1-3
11   1 Peter 2:1-3

destined for "mature manhood." The young men who were entrusted with the Gospel and given the task of initiating the Great Commission were pregnant with vision for this maturity. This was the standard upon which the epistles were written, and two thousand years later, still beckon us to bear—that the Church has been appointed to share in the fellowship of Christ's sufferings by being conformed into the image of Him who sacrificially bled and died.

In Philippians 3, Paul defines this as the apostolic standard to which the Church is called, saying that he "counted all things as loss" for the sake of "gaining Christ" and that he desired nothing more than to "know Him and the power of His resurrection, and [to] *share His sufferings*, becoming *like Him in His death.*" Then, in verses 14-15, after emphasizing the issues of loss, suffering, and death, He said that he "presses on" to gain the "prize of the upward call of God in Christ Jesus." Furthermore, Paul charges the Philippians saying, "*let those who are mature think this way.*" For Paul, the journey into maturity was the road of death and resurrection. It was in the fellowship of suffering. Christ was his life, and death was gain. These weren't just words or hyperboles; they were convictions that ultimately cost him his life. A short time after those words were penned, he was brutally executed by a Roman blade. While some may view such a thing as a tragic end to a happy life, Paul declares that it is the standard of Christian maturity. Therefore I agree with Hovey who wrote that

> the Christian life [is] an adventure of faith that is rooted in the church's witness to the world. As such, martyrdom is not witness gone terribly wrong but its ultimate paradigm. Martyrs have not failed in their proclamation; their deaths are found within the very substance of the gospel proclaimed. This is the gospel proclaimed by all Christians

who include in their proclamation the work of remembering those who have died in their witness. To take part in this work and this witness is therefore to acknowledge that "martyr-church" identifies the locus of Christian life for all who follow Christ.[12]

While this theological paradigm is met with scoffing by some, it is, nonetheless, entirely biblical. Many of the epistles (and at least one of the Gospels) were written with the intended purpose of strengthening the saints in their struggle as a martyr-Church suffering the scourge of persecution. In light of that struggle, Peter also commanded the early Church (echoing Paul) saying, "Since therefore Christ suffered in the flesh, *arm yourselves with the same way of thinking.*"[13] The command to "arm yourselves with the same way of thinking" displayed by Christ when He willingly "suffered in the flesh" must be proclaimed in order for the Church to "be built up" into "mature manhood" and the "full stature of Christ" as we are exhorted in Ephesians. Like Jesus in Revelation 2, Peter wanted the Church to embrace a theology of martyrdom, and the call to be faithful unto death. This, I believe, is integral to the biblical theology of Christian maturity and essential for the Church, against whom the gates of hell will not prevail. Whether or not *we* are willing to embrace that "same way of thinking" that Christ demonstrated when He suffered in the flesh, it is clear that the Church in the first century was. It was a hallmark of those who followed "the Way,"[14] as they counted it a privilege to express their devotion to Jesus in the fiery

---

12 Craig Hovey, *To Share in the Body: A Theology of Martyrdom for Today's Church,* 18-19.

13 1 Peter 4:1

14 "The Way" was a name used by the early Christian community for itself (Acts 9:2; 18:26; 19:9, 23; 22:4; 24:14, 22).

cauldron of persecution. With Jesus' call to "lose their lives" ringing in their ears, and the revelation of His glory burning in their hearts, they joyfully obeyed their Master, even "unto death." Two thousand years later, can we recognize that this call is still unchanged, and that we too, are called to walk that same narrow road?

A BRIDE MADE READY

While this theology has had a central role in the life of the corporate Church throughout the entirety of Church history, it will have its fullest expression at the end of the age. History is moving toward an appointed consummation unto which the wife of the Lamb will "make herself ready." While John was on the island of Patmos, he was given a glimpse of the Church's end-time maturity in context to that great consummation. He explained what he saw saying,

> Then I heard what seemed to be the voice of a great multitude, like the roar of many waters and like the sound of mighty peals of thunder, crying out,
> "Hallelujah!
> For the Lord our God
> the Almighty reigns.
> Let us rejoice and exult
> and give him the glory,
> for the marriage of the Lamb has come,
> and his Bride has made herself ready;
> it was granted her to clothe herself
> with fine linen, bright and pure"—
> for the fine linen is the righteous deeds of the saints.
> (Revelation 19:6-8)

Whether we know it or not, history is moving towards the climactic event of that awesome Day—the union of the Bride with her heavenly Bridegroom. As surely as that Day will come, so too will the Church fulfill her destiny of maturity, in order that she may be presented as a Bride who has made herself ready. Like Queen Esther, the Bride of Christ will be prepared until she is bright and pure, "without spot or wrinkle"—wholly fit for her King.

How glorious is the thought that the book of Revelation ends with a wedding and a joyous celebration, especially when we consider that three of the most dominant subjects throughout the book are (1) the rage of Satan, (2) the temporal judgments of God, and (3) the violent persecution of the saints. Herein lies an essential end-time paradigm. At the end of the age, in context to the greatest expression of Satan's wrath and God's judgments, the Church will experience the greatest suffering she has ever known. Yet the outcome of this great and terrible crisis will be the glorious scene that John describes in chapter 19—the Bride will be ready to meet her Maker and her Husband. And the two shall evermore be one.

Inasmuch as we ought to celebrate the triumphant end of the story, we must understand that which precedes it. For what precedes it is the very thing that prepares the Bride for that glorious Day. This is why the book of Revelation is essential reading for the end-time Church. In vivid detail it describes how the saints who are alive in the generation of His appearing will be persecuted and how they are to respond. This message must be proclaimed universally before the final tribulation so as to prepare the people of God for our crucible.

The Blood of the Lamb, and the Blood of the Saints

With these things in view, let us return again to Revelation 12:11 and consider how we are to prepare for and respond to the coming scourge. Describing the saints in the fiery furnace of the "great tribulation," John wrote that

> they have conquered him by the blood of the Lamb and by the word of their testimony, for they loved not their lives even unto death. (Revelation 12:11)

The passage has four parts to it, and it is important to understand all four and how they relate to each other. First, we read the central proposition: *the saints will conquer Satan*. Second, we read of how they will prevail: *by the blood of the Lamb*. Third, we read of another way they will prevail: *by the word of their testimony*. And fourth, we read the ground clause: *for they loved not their lives even unto death*. To rightly understand and apply the four components of this text, we need to take note of the reoccurring word, "they." This word emphasizes the corporate expression of the spirit of martyrdom and gives us a picture of what Jesus meant in chapter 2 when He exhorted Smyrna to be "faithful unto death."

Victory over Satan, and faithfulness to God (especially in the generation of the Lord's return) may require bloodshed. If this were not true, it would not be a point of *reoccurring emphasis* in the book of Revelation. "Blood" is at the heart of this incredible book—the blood of the Lamb, and the blood of the saints. *Salvation* is found in the blood of the Lamb alone. And upon this truth rests the *word of our testimony*. But *maturity*—which is intended to follow salvation—is found in *not loving our lives unto death*. Jesus has a higher vision for the Church than mere salvation through His blood (as amazing as that is). He purchased us with His blood so that we could express our devotion to Him by the shedding of ours (should it be granted to us).

It can and must be shown that a walk worthy of the calling for which we were saved is centered around the call to surrender our spirits into the hands of He who bled for us, and to submit our lives to His will at any cost, even "unto death." This is the way the end-time Church will follow Christ—by being "conformed into His image"[15] and "becoming like Him in His death."[16]

The Church's final triumph over Satan is sure. This purpose cannot fail. Our great foe will soon be vanquished. When Jesus shed His blood, He secured our enemy's ultimate demise. But there is more to the story. It is our submission to the crucifying will of God, to the radical extent that we love not our lives even unto death, that our victory over the Accuser is materialized at the end of this present evil age. I believe that it can be proven by a simple exegesis of Revelation 12:7-11 that the Church's posture towards Satan in that hour through the embrace of martyrdom will be an act of spiritual warfare that plays a decisive role in his eviction from heaven[17] and the provocation of his final outburst of bitter vitriol against the saints.[18]

Some are content to emphasize the message of a victorious Church apart from the Gospel of Jesus' blood and the call to faithfulness unto death. They avoid subjects like the wrath of God, the sin of man, the necessity of Christ's vicarious suffering, and the issue of martyrdom. But this is a deficient Gospel. We desperately

---

15 Romans 8:29
16 Philippians 3:10-11
17 Job 1 and Zechariah 3 tell us that Satan has access to the courts of heaven. Paul spoke of him as "the prince of the power of the air" (Ephesians 2:2) and "the god of this age" (2 Corinthians 4:4). He currently maintains a temporary position of authority in "heavenly places" (Ephesians 6:12). During the final tribulation, he will be displaced from this position before his ultimate demise.
18 Some teach that Revelation 12 describes the historical eviction of Satan from heaven asserting the idea that this event has already happened. However, the text and its context make it clear that this is a future eschatological event that occurs during the "great tribulation" (Revelation 7:14; Matthew 24:15-31; Daniel 12:1-7).

need the "full counsel of God."[19] The apostolic Gospel is predicated on these core realities, and the New Testament is pregnant with them, and we must be faithful to proclaim them. Our victory over the Devil *requires* it. But proclaiming these things is not enough in itself; they must be *demonstrated*. Our victory over Satan will be determined largely by whether or not we have actually surrendered our lives into the hands of our Lord. For many, such surrender may be unto death. Read what John heard Jesus say in response to the martyrs of the final generation who were crying out for Jesus' intervention in the face of the mounting atrocity.

> When he opened the fifth seal, I saw under the altar the souls of those who had been slain for the word of God and for the witness they had borne. They cried out with a loud voice, "O Sovereign Lord, holy and true, how long before You will judge and avenge our blood on those who dwell on the earth?" Then they were each given a white robe and told to rest a little longer, until the number of their fellow servants and their brothers should be complete, who were to be killed as they themselves had been. (Revelation 6:9-11)

This is an incredible picture. "Those who had been slain" are standing before Jesus in the place of intercession asking that their blood be "avenged." Filled with holy passion, John saw them standing before the King requesting that He intervene and bring an end to the bloody scourge that claimed their lives. To this Jesus responds saying, "Not yet." That is, not until the full "number" of saints are "killed as they themselves had been." There in Revelation 6:9-11 is one of the clearest pictures of the Church growing into corporate maturity through martyrdom. As the Devil unleashes his final fury at the end of the age, the blood of the saints will flow as they are slain en masse.

19   Acts 20:27

But as it was in the crucifixion of Jesus, by taking their lives, Satan hastens *his own* demise.[20]

Faithful Unto Death

The Church's maturity and ultimate victory over the Evil One is contingent upon our embrace of the call to martyrdom: to be "faithful unto death" *together*. To casually dismiss this issue as fringe or irrelevant is to turn our backs on a multitude of exhortations and prophecies concerning the call to count all things as loss—even our lives—for the sake of gaining Christ. This message is not only integral to the apostolic Gospel, it is indispensable to the Church being "built up" into "mature manhood."

20 Revelation 12:11

CONCLUSION
THOSE OF WHOM THE WORLD IS NOT WORTHY

The Church at the end of the age will resemble the Church at the start through the expression of her devotion to Jesus and her martyr-witness to the nations. In light of the call to martyrdom in the New Testament, its prominence in Church history, and its place in God's age-ending purposes, the biblical theological foundation of this assertion is undeniably firm, regardless of what our contemporary Christian culture may tell us.

Those whose lives and ministries are driven by this conviction will change the world. More importantly, they will be counted among that precious company of saints who "by grace" and "through faith" lived in such a way as to be esteemed as those "of whom the world is not worthy."[1]

Therefore, Church, for the joy set before us, let us lay our lives on the altar of His will and lift our voices to declare with

1   Hebrews 11:32-40

those in Paradise, "Worthy is the Lamb!"[2] so that "with full courage now as always, Christ will be honored in our bodies, whether by life or by death. For to us to live is Christ, and to die is gain."[3]

2   Revelation 5:9-10
3   Philippians 1:20-21

"A Trumpet Call" by John G. Lake[1]

The thirteenth chapter of Acts tells us the story of the ordination and sending forth of the apostle Paul, his ordination to the apostleship. Paul never writes of himself until after the thirteenth chapter of Acts. He had been an evangelist and teacher for thirteen years when the thirteenth chapter of Acts was written, and the ordination took place that is recorded there. Men who have a real call are not afraid of apprenticeships.

There is a growing up in experience in the ministry. When Paul started out in the ministry he was definitely called of God and was assured of God through Ananias that it would not be an easy service but a terrific one, for God said to Ananias:

> Arise and go into the street which is called Straight and inquire, in the house of Judas, for one called Saul of Tarsus, for behold, he is praying. He is a chosen vessel unto Me, to bear My Name before the gentiles, and kings, and the children of Israel: For I will show him how great things he must suffer for My Name's sake.

1   Roberts Liardon, *John G. Lake: The Complete Collection of His Life Teachings,* (New Kensington PA: Whitaker House, 1999), 36-41.

That is what Jesus Christ, the crucified and the glorified Son of God, told Ananias to say to the apostle Paul. He was not going to live in a holy ecstasy and wear a beautiful halo, and have a heavenly time, and ride in a limousine. He was going to have a drastic time, a desperate struggle, and a terrific experience. And no man in biblical history ever had more dreadful things to endure than the apostle Paul. He gives a list, in his second letter to the Corinthians, of the things he had endured.

> Of the Jews five times received I forty stripes save one. Thrice I was beaten with rods. Once I was stoned, thrice I suffered shipwreck, a night and a day have I been in the deep; in journeying often, in perils of waters, in perils of the heathen, in perils in the city, in perils in the wilderness, in perils in the sea, in perils among false brethren. In weariness and painfulness, in watching often, in hunger and thirst, in fasting often, in cold and nakedness.

They stripped him of his clothing, and the executioner lashed him with an awful scourge, until bleeding and lacerated and broken, he fell helpless, and unconscious and insensible, then they doused him with a bucket of salt water to keep the maggots off, and threw him into a cell to recover. That was the price of apostleship! That was the price of the call of God and His service. But God said, "He shall bear My Name before the gentiles and kings, and the children of Israel." He qualified as God's messenger.

Beloved, we have lost the character of consecration here manifested. God is trying to restore it in our day. He has not been able to make such progress with the average preacher on that line. All too often, it is, "Mrs. So and So said so and so, and I am just not going to take it!" That is the kind of preacher, with another kind of call; not the heavenly call; not the God call; not the death call if necessary. That is not the kind the apostle Paul was, or was called to be.

Do you know why God poured out His Spirit in South Africa like He did no where else in the world? There was a reason. This example will illustrate. We had one hundred and twenty-five men out on the field at one time. We were a very young institution and were not known in the world. South Africa is seven thousand miles from any European country. It is ten thousand miles by way of England to the United States. Our finances got so low, under the awful assault we were compelled to endure, that there came a time I could not even mail to these workers, at the end of the month, a $10 bill. It got so I could not send them $2. The situation was desperate. What was I to do? Under these circumstances I did not want to take the responsibility of leaving men and their families on the frontier without real knowledge of what the conditions were.

Some of us at headquarters sold our clothes in some cases, sold certain pieces of furniture out of the house, sold anything we could sell, to bring those hundred and twenty-five workers off the field for a conference.

One night in the progress of the conference I was invited by a committee to leave the room for a minute or two. The conference wanted to have a word by themselves. So I stepped out to a restaurant for a cup of coffee, and came back. When I came back in, I found they had rearranged the chairs in an oval, with a little table at one end, and on the table was the bread and wine. Old Father Vanderwall, speaking for the company said, "Brother John, during your absence we have come to a conclusion. We have made our decision. We want you to serve the LORD's Supper. We are going back to our fields. We are going back if our wives die. We are going back if we have to starve. We are going back if we have to walk back. We are going back if our children die. We are going back if we die ourselves. We have but one request. If we die, we want you to come and bury us."

The next year I buried twelve of those men, along with sixteen of their wives and children.

In my judgment, not one of them, if they had a few things a white man needs to eat, could but what might have lived. Friends, when you want to find out why the power of God came down from heaven in South Africa like it never came down before, since the time of the apostles, there is your answer.

Jesus Christ put the spirit of martyrdom in the ministry. Jesus instituted His ministry with a pledge unto death. When He was with the disciples on the last night, He took the cup, "when He drank, saying." Beloved, the "saying" was the significant thing. It was Jesus Christ's pledge to the twelve who stood with Him, "This cup is the New Testament in my blood." Then He said, "Drink ye all of it!"

Friends, those who were there and drank to that pledge, of Jesus Christ, entered into the same covenant and purpose that he did. That is what all the pledges mean. Men have pledged themselves in the same cup from time immemorial. Generals have pledged their armies unto death. It has been a custom in the human race. Jesus Christ sanctified it to the Church forever, bless God!

"My blood in the New Testament... Drink all of it!" Let us become one. Let us become one in our purpose to die for the world. Your blood and mine together. "My blood is the New Testament." That is my demand from you. It is your high privilege!

Dear friends, there is not an authentic history that can tell us whether any one of them died a natural death. We know that at least nine of them were martyrs, possibly all. Peter died on a cross, James was beheaded. For Thomas they did not even wait to make a cross they nailed him to an olive tree. John was sentenced to be executed at Ephesus by putting him in a cauldron of boiling oil, God delivered him, and his executioners refused to repeat the operation, and he was banished to the Isle of Patmos. John thought so little about it that he never even tells of the incident. He says, "I was in the Isle called Patmos, for the Word of God, and for the testimony of Jesus Christ." That was explanation enough. He had committed himself to Jesus Christ for life or death.

Friends, the group of missionaries that followed me went without food, and went without clothes, and once when one of my preachers was sunstruck, and had wandered away, I tracked him by the blood marks of his feet. Another time I was hunting for one of my missionaries, a young Englishman, twenty-two years of age. He had come from a line of Church of England preachers for five hundred years. When I arrived at the native village the old native chief said, "He is not here. He went over the mountains, and you know him, he is a white man and he has not learned to walk barefooted."

That is the kind of consecration that established Pentecost in South Africa. That is the reason we have a hundred thousand native Christians in South Africa. That is the reason we have 1250 native preachers. That is the reason we have 350 white churches in South Africa. That is the reason that, today, we are the most rapidly growing Church in South Africa!

I am not persuading you, dear friends, by holding out a hope that the way is going to be easy. I am calling you, in the Name of Jesus Christ, you dear ones who expect to be ordained to the Gospel of Jesus Christ, tonight, take the route that Jesus took. The route the early Church took. The victory route, whether by life or death. Historians declare, "The blood of the martyrs was the seed of her church." Beloved, that is what the difficulty is in our day, we have so little seed. The Church needs more martyr blood.

If I were pledging men and women to the Gospel of the Son of God, as I am endeavoring to do tonight, it would not be to have a nice Church and harmonious surroundings and a sweet do-nothing time. I would invite them to be ready to die. That was the spirit of early Methodism. John Wesley established a heroic call. He demanded every preacher to be "ready to pray, ready to preach, ready to die." That is always the spirit of Christianity. There is another spirit that has come into the Church, it is not the spirit of Christianity. It is a foreign spirit. It is a sissified substitute.

I lived on corn meal mush many a period with my family, and we did not growl, and I preached to thousands of people, not colored people but white people. When my missionaries were on the field existing on corn meal mush, I could not eat pie. My heart was joined with them. That is the reason we never had splits in our work in South Africa. It is one country where Pentecost never split. This split business began to develop years afterward, when pumpkin pie eating Pentecostal missionaries began infesting the country. Men who are ready to die for the Son of Man do not split! They do not holler the first time they get a stomach ache.

Bud Robinson tells a story of himself. He went to preach in the southern mountains. It was the first time in his life that no one invited him to go home with them and eat. So he slept on the floor, and the next night, and the next night. After five days and five nights had passed, and his stomach began to growl for food terribly, every once in a while he would stop and say, "Lay down, you brute!", and he went out with his sermon. That is what won. That is what will win every time. That is what we need today. We need men who are willing to get off the highway. When I started to preach the Gospel I walked twenty miles on Sunday morning to my service and walked home twenty miles in the night when I got through. I did it for years for Jesus and souls.

In early Methodism an old local preacher would start Saturday and walk all night, and then walk all night Sunday night to get back to his work. It was the common custom. Peter Cartwright preached for sixty dollars per year, and baptized ten thousand converts.

Friends, we talk about consecration, and we preach about consecration but that is the kind of consecration that my heart is asking for tonight. That is the kind of consecration that will get answers from heaven. That is the kind of pledge God will honor. That is the kind of consecration to which I would pledge Pentecost. I would strip Pentecost of its frills and follies.

Jesus Christ, through the Holy Ghost, calls us tonight, not to an earthly mansion and a ten thousand dollar motor car, but to put our lives, body and soul and spirit, on the altar of service. All hail! Ye who are ready to die for Christ and the glorious Pentecostal Gospel. We salute you! You are brothers with us and with your Lord.

The challenge of the unoccupied fields of the world is one to great faith and, therefore, to great sacrifice. Our willingness to sacrifice for an enterprise is always in proportion to our faith in that enterprise. Faith has the genius of transforming the barely possible into actuality. Once men are dominated by the conviction that a thing must be done, they will stop at nothing until it is accomplished. We have our "marching orders," as the Iron Duke [Arthur Wesley, Duke of Wellington] said, and because our Commander-in-Chief is not absent, but with us, the impossible becomes not only practical but imperative. Charles Spurgeon, preaching from the text, "All power is given unto Me. Lo I am with you always," used these words: "You have a factor here that is absolutely infinite, and what does it matter as to what other factors may be. 'I will do as much as I can,' says one. Any fool can do that. He that believes in Christ does

1   Samuel Zwemer, *The Unoccupied Mission Fields of Africa and Asia,* (The Student Volunteer Movement; 1st Edition, 1911).

what he can not do, attempts the impossible and performs it."

Frequent set-backs and apparent failure never dishearten the real pioneer. Occasional martyrdoms are only a fresh incentive. Opposition is a stimulus to greater activity. Great victory has never been possible without great sacrifice. If the winning of Port Arthur required human bullets, we cannot expect to carry the Port Arthurs and Gibraltars of the non-Christian world without loss of life. Does it really matter how many die or how much money we spend in opening closed doors, and in occupying the different fields, if we really believe that missions are warfare and that the King's Glory is at stake? War always means blood and treasure. Our only concern should be to keep the fight aggressive and to win victory regardless of cost or sacrifice. The unoccupied fields of the world must have their Calvary before they can have their Pentecost. Raymond Lull, the first missionary to the Moslem world, expressed the same thought in medieval language when he wrote: "As a hungry man makes dispatch and takes large morsels on account of his great hunger, so Thy servant feels a great desire to die that he may glorify Thee. He hurries day and night to complete his work in order that he may give up his blood and his tears to be shed for Thee."

"An Inverted Homesickness"

The unoccupied fields of the world await those who are willing to be lonely for the sake of Christ. To the pioneer missionary, the words of our Lord Jesus Christ to the apostles when He showed them His hands and His feet, come with special force: "As my Father hath sent Me, even so send I you" (John 20:21). He came into the world, and it was a great unoccupied mission field. "He came unto His own, and His own received

Him not" (John 1:11). He came and His welcome was deri-
sion, His life suffering, and His throne the Cross. As He came,
He expects us to go. We must follow in His footprints. The
pioneer missionary, in overcoming obstacles and difficulties,
has the privilege not only of knowing Christ and the power
of His resurrection, but also something of the fellowship of
His suffering. For the people of Tibet or Somaliland, Mongolia
or Afghanistan, Arabia or Nepal, the Sudan or Abyssinia, he
may be called to say with Paul, "Now I rejoice in my sufferings for you and fill to the brim the penury of the afflictions
of Christ in my flesh for His body's sake which is the Church"
(Greek text, Col. 1:24; cf. Luke 21:4 and Mark 12:44). What is
it but the glory of the impossible! Who would naturally prefer
to leave the warmth and comfort of hearth and home and the
love of the family circle to go after a lost sheep, whose cry we
have faintly heard in the howling of the tempest? Yet such is
the glory of the task that neither home-ties nor home needs
can hold back those who have caught the vision and the spirit
of the Great Shepherd. Because the lost ones are His sheep,
and He has made us His shepherds and not His hirelings, we
must bring them back.

> Although the road be rough and steep, I go to the desert to
> find my sheep.

"There is nothing finer nor more pathetic to me," says Dr.
Forsyth, "than the way in which missionaries unlearn the love
of the old home, die to their native land, and wed their hearts
to the people they have served and won; so that they cannot
rest in England but must return to lay their bones where they
spent their hearts for Christ. How vulgar the common patrio-
tisms seem beside this inverted home-sickness, this passion

of a kingdom which has no frontiers and no favored race, the passion of a homeless Christ!"

James Gilmour in Mongolia, David Livingstone in Central Africa, Grenfell on the Congo, Keith Falconer in Arabia, Dr. Rijnhart and Miss Annie Taylor in Tibet, Chalmers in New Guinea, Morrison in China, Henry Martyn in Persia, and all the others like them had this "inverted home-sickness," this passion to call that country their home which was most in need of the Gospel. In this passion all other passions died; before this vision all other visions faded; this call drowned all other voices. They were the pioneers of the Kingdom, the fore-lopers of God, eager to cross the border-marches and discover new lands or win new empires.

THE PIONEER SPIRIT

These forelopers of God went not with hatchet and brand, but with the Sword of the Spirit and with the Belt of Truth. They went and blazed the way for those that followed after. Their scars were the seal of their apostleship, and they gloried also in tribulation.

Like the pioneer apostle, "always bearing about in the body the dying of the Lord Jesus, and approving themselves as ministers of God in stripes, in imprisonments, in tumults, in watching, in fasting."

Thomas Valpy French, Bishop of Lahore, whom Dr. Eugene Stock called "the most distinguished of all Church Missionary Society missionaries," had the real pioneer spirit and knew the glory of the impossible. After forty years of labors abundant and fruitful in India, he resigned his bishopric and planned to reach the interior of Arabia with the Gospel. He was an intellectual and spiritual giant. "To live with him was to drink in an atmosphere that was spiritually bracing. As the air of the Engadine (a favorite tourist ground in Switzerland) is to the body, so was his intimacy to the soul. It was an education to be with him. There was nothing that he thought a man should not yield – home or wife or health if God's call was apparent. But then every one knew that he only asked of them what he himself had done and was always doing." And when Mackay, of Uganda, in his remarkable plea for a mission to the Arabs of Oman called for "half a dozen young men, the pick of the English universities, to make the venture in faith," this lion-hearted veteran of sixty-six years responded alone. It was the glory of the impossible. Yet from Muscat he wrote shortly before his death:

> If I can get no faithful servant and guide for the journey into the interior, well versed in dealing with Arabs and getting needful common supplies (I want but little), I may try Bahrein, or Hodeidah and Sana, and if that fails, the north of Africa again, in some highland; for without a house of our own the climate would be insufferable for me – at least during the very hot months – and one's work would be at a standstill. But I shall not give up, please God, even temporarily, my plans for the interior, unless, all avenues being closed, it would be sheer madness to attempt to carry them out.

"I shall not give up" – and he did not till he died. Nor will the Church of Christ give up the work for which he and others like him laid down their lives in Oman. It goes on.

THE APOSTOLIC AMBITION

The unoccupied provinces of Arabia and the Sudan await men with the spirit of Bishop French. For the ambition to reach out from centers already occupied to regions beyond, even when those very centers are undermanned and in need of reinforcement, is not Quixotic or fantastic, but truly apostolic. "Yes, so have I been ambitious," said Paul, "to preach the Gospel not where Christ was already named, lest I should build on another man's foundation; but as it is written, they shall see to whom no tidings of Him came, and they who have not heard shall understand" (Romans 15:20-21). He wrote this when leaving a city as important as Corinth, and goes on to state that this is the reason why he did not yet visit Rome, but that he hopes to do so on his way to Spain! If the uttermost confines of the Roman Empire were part of his program who had already preached Christ from Jerusalem to Illyricum in the first century, we surely, at the beginning of the twentieth century, should have no less ambition to enter every unoccupied field that "they may see to whom no tidings came and that those who have not heard may understand."

"There is no instance of an apostle being driven abroad under the compulsion of a bald command. Each one went as a lover to his betrothed on his appointed errand. It was all instinctive and natural. They were equally controlled by the common vision, but they had severally personal visions which drew them whither they were needed. In the first days of Christianity, there is an absence of the calculating spirit. Most of the apostles died outside of Palestine, though human logic would have forbidden them to leave the country until it had been Christianized. The calculating instinct is death to faith, and had the apostles allowed it to control their motives and actions, they would have said: 'The need in Jerusalem is so profound, our responsibilities to people of our own blood so obvious, that we must live up to the principle that charity begins at home. After we have won the people of Jerusalem, of Judea and of the Holy Land in general, then it will be time enough to go abroad; but our problems, political, moral and religious, are so unsolved here in this one spot that it is manifestly absurd to bend our shoulders to a new load.'"

It was the bigness of the task and its difficulty that thrilled the early Church. Its apparent impossibility was its glory, its world-wide character its grandeur. The same is true today.

"I am happy," wrote Neesima of Japan, "in a meditation on the marvelous growth of Christianity in the world, and believe that if it finds any obstacles it will advance still faster and swifter even as the stream runs faster when it finds any hindrances on its course."

HOPE AND PATIENCE

He that ploweth the virgin soil should plow in hope. God never disappoints His husbandmen. The harvest always follows the seed time. "When we first came to our field," writes missionary Hogberg from Central Asia, "it was impossible to gather even a few people to hear the glad tidings of the Gospel. We could not gather any children for school. We could not spread gospels or tracts. When building the new station, we also had a little chapel built. Then we wondered, will this room ever be filled up with Moslems listening to the Gospel? Our little chapel has been filled with hearers and still a larger room! Day after day we may preach as much as we have strength to, and the Moslems no longer object to listen to the Gospel truth. 'Before your coming hither no one spoke or thought of Jesus Christ, now everywhere one hears His name,' a Mohammedan said to me. At the beginning of our work they threw away the Gospels or burnt them, or brought them back again – now they buy them, kiss the books, and touching it to the forehead and pressing it to the heart, they show the highest honor that a Moslem can show a book."

But the pioneer husbandman must have long patience. When Judson was lying loaded with chains in a Burmese dungeon, a fellow prisoner asked with a sneer about the prospect for the conversion of the heathen. Judson calmly answered, "The prospects are as bright as are the promises of God." There is scarcely a country today which is not as accessible, or where the difficulties are greater, than was the case in Burma when Judson faced them and overcame.

Challenge of the Closed Door

The prospects for the evangelization of all the unoccupied fields are "as bright as the promises of God." Why should we longer wait to evangelize them? "The evangelization of the world in this generation is no play-word," says Robert E. Spencer. "It is no motto to be bandied about carelessly. The evangelization of the world in this generation is the summons of Jesus Christ to every one of the disciples to lay himself upon a cross, himself to walk in the footsteps of Him who, though He was rich, for our sakes became poor, that we through His poverty might be rich, himself to count his life as of no account, that he may spend it as Christ spent His for the redemption of the world." Who will do this for the unoccupied fields? The student volunteers of today must not rest satisfied until the watchword, peculiarly their own, finds practical application for the most neglected and difficult fields, as well as the countries where the harvest is ripe and the call is for reapers in ever increasing numbers. The plea of destitution is even stronger than that of opportunity. Opportunism is not the last word in missions. The open door beckons; the closed door challenges him who has a right to enter. The unoccupied fields of the world have, therefore, a claim of peculiar weight and urgency. "In this twentieth century of Christian history there should be no unoccupied fields. The Church is bound to remedy the lamentable condition with the least possible delay."

MAKE A LIFE, NOT A LIVING

The unoccupied fields, therefore, are a challenge to all whose lives are unoccupied by that which is highest and best; whose lives are occupied only with the weak things or the base things that do not count. There are eyes that have never been illumined by a great vision, minds that have never been gripped by an unselfish thought, hearts that have never thrilled with passion for another's wrong, and hands that have never grown weary or strong in lifting a great burden. To such the knowledge of these Christless millions in lands yet unoccupied should come like a new call from Macedonia, and a startling vision of God's will for them. As Bishop Brent remarks, "We never know what measure of moral capacity is at our disposal until we try to express it in action. An adventure of some proportions is not uncommonly all that a young man needs to determine and fix his manhood's powers." Is there a more heroic test for the powers of manhood than pioneer work in the mission field? Here is opportunity for those who at home may never find elbow-room for their latent capacities, who may never find adequate scope elsewhere for all the powers of their minds and their souls. There are hundreds of Christian college men who expect to spend life in practicing law or in some trade for a livelihood, yet who have strength and talent enough to enter these unoccupied fields. There are young doctors who might gather around them in some new mission station thousands of those who "suffer the horrors of heathenism and Islam," and lift their burden of pain, but who now confine their efforts to some "pent-up Utica" where the healing art is subject to the law of competition and is measured too often merely in terms of a cash-book and ledger. They are making a living; they might be making a life.

Bishop Phillips Brooks once threw down the challenge of a big task in these words: "Do not pray for easy lives; pray to be stronger men. Do not pray for tasks equal to your powers; pray for powers equal to your tasks. Then the doing of your work shall be no miracle, but you shall be a miracle." He could not have chosen words more applicable if he had spoken of the evangelization of the unoccupied fields of the world with all their baffling difficulties and their glorious impossibilities. God can give us power for the task. He was sufficient for those who went out in the past, and is sufficient for those who go out today.

Face to face with these millions in darkness and degradation, knowing the condition of their lives on the unimpeachable testimony of those who have visited these countries, this great unfinished task, this unattempted task, calls today for those who are willing to endure and suffer in accomplishing it.

No Sacrifice, But a Privilege

When David Livingstone visited Cambridge University, on December 4, 1857, he made an earnest appeal for that continent, which was then almost wholly an unoccupied field. His words, which were in a sense his last will and testament for college men, as regards Africa, may well close this book:

> For my own part, I have never ceased to rejoice that God has appointed me to such an office. People talk of the sacrifice

I have made in spending so much of my life in Africa. Can that be called a sacrifice which is simply paid back as a small part of a great debt owing to our God, which we can never repay? Is that a sacrifice which brings its own blest reward in healthful activity, the consciousness of doing good, peace of mind, and a bright hope of a glorious destiny hereafter? Away with the word in such a view, and with such a thought! It is emphatically no sacrifice. Say rather it is a privilege. Anxiety, sickness, suffering, or danger, now and then, with a foregoing of the common conveniences and charities of this life, may make us pause, and cause the spirit to waver, and the soul to sink, but let this only be for a moment. All these are nothing when compared with the glory which shall hereafter be revealed in and for us. I never made a sacrifice. I beg to direct your attention to Africa. I know that in a few years I shall be cut off in that country, which is now open; do not let it be shut again! I go back to Africa to try to make an open path for commerce and Christianity; do you carry out the work which I have begun? I leave it with you.

Appendix III
"Don't Complicate the 'Missionary Call'" [1]
by David Sitton [2]

I chuckle when I hear missionaries say they "surrendered to the call" of ministry. I always want to ask, "After you surrendered, were you waterboarded, or just hauled off in handcuffs and leg irons?" Was it really necessary for you to be abducted by a heavenly vision before you would go joyfully into the work of the Gospel in unreached places?

The missionary call is not like a prison dog that tracks us down, sniffs us out, and hog-ties us for the nations. That kind of talk bugs me! It's bad theology. Nowhere in Scripture is a "mysterious (supernatural) call" a prerequisite before we can respond to the Great Commission. The opposite is actually true.

1 David Sitton, "Don't Complicate the Missionary Call," *To Every Tribe* (website), accessed 2011, http://66.132.241.23/uploads/Dont_Complicate_the_Call.pdf.
2 For more information about David Sitton and *To Every Tribe* ministries, visit: http://www.toeverytribe.com.

Don't Wait for a Call

No aspect of mission is more bogged down with extra-biblical baggage than the "Missionary Call." The clear command of Christ "to go" should be, by itself, sufficient to set you on your way to unreached regions.

You can't go wrong by trying to go. Be aggressive to go. The Lord will direct your moving feet.

Do you know how 99% of the cross-cultural workers for the Gospel in the book of Acts got to the unreached places? In a detailed missiological study of the book of Acts, Bob Sjogren breaks it down for us.

- 99% of the missionaries in Acts went cross-cultural because of one reason: Persecution.

What About the Other 1%?

- 74% served cross-culturally because the apostle Paul challenged them to go.
    - 18% went because their local churches sent them.
    - 7% went simply because of their zeal and desire to do it![3]

Dramatic calls to ministry are the exception. If you have it in your heart to go, then go. And lean on the sovereignty of God to get you where He wants you in the harvest.

Try to Go

Paul tried to go into Asia, but the Lord wouldn't let him. He then tried to go to Bithynia, but "the Holy Spirit forbade him." Still, he kept trying to go. I count at least six cities in Acts 16:1-6 where Paul tried to take the Gospel. It was only then that the

---

3   Bill and Amy Stearns, *Run With The Vision*, (Bethany House Publishers), 125-126.

Lord gave him a vision of the Macedonian. He woke up the next morning and immediately headed for the regions north. The point? Get radical with the going and God will get radical in the specific guiding.

I was never called to be a missionary. I wasn't drafted. I volunteered. No special call was needed. I chose to go. I want to go. I am compelled to go. Where I go is determined by an open Bible (Romans 15:20-21) and a stretched-out map of unreached regions where Jesus isn't known. Going for Jesus and with Jesus to the ends of the Earth is the privilege of a lifetime.

ABOUT THE AUTHOR

Dalton Thomas is married with two sons. He is a Bible teacher and pioneer missionary focused on calling, training, and mobilizing laborers for frontier ministry. For more information and free resources, visit *daltonthomas.org*.

ALSO BY DALTON THOMAS

The Controversy of Zion and the Time of Jacob's Trouble

MASKILIM PUBLISHING

ꭑꝓ *Mission Statement:* We are committed to printing, promoting, and distributing resources to inform, strengthen, and prepare the Church among the nations before the return of the Lord. Maskilim Publishing is based in Tauranga, New Zealand.

website: *www.maskilimpublishing.com*